What Will We Make?
What Can We Do?

Art Activities, Games and Action Rhymes for Ages 3 Through 6

Mary and Herb Montgomery

Winston Press

a division of Franciscan Communications
Los Angeles, California

Authors: Mary and Herb Montgomery
Editor: Carrie Leadingham
Designer: Nancy Condon
Illustrators:
    Cover and section dividers: Kathy Rogers
    Activity pages: Sally King Brewer

Send all inquiries to:
Franciscan Communications
1229 South Santee Street
Los Angeles, California 90015

Printed in the United States of America

ISBN: 1-55944-015-5

96 95 94 93 92 10 9 8 7 6 5 4 3 2 1

CONTENTS

Introduction

How to Use This Book

What Will We Make? What Can We Do? was developed for teachers and parents who are looking for art activities, games and action rhymes that capture the interest of the three to six-year-old child. The art activities included in this book call for materials that are easily available wherever school supplies are sold, or in the average household. Many of the materials used would otherwise be discarded!

The activities can be done with minimum fuss and maximum creativity. Activity Extensions are given to make each activity appropriate for children with more advanced skills or to lengthen the activity for an extended session. The games are fun without being highly competitive, and the action rhymes delight children with their rhythm and imagery.

Teachers in a church school, or other alternative educational setting, typically use programs that are designed for an hour session. If your class lasts longer than an hour, or you want alternative activities besides the ones provided in your lesson plans, this book will be an excellent resource. Alphabetical indexes are located at the beginning of each section. (See Table of Contents.) A topical index at the beginning of the Art Activities section correlates activities with themes commonly covered in early childhood programs. Because of this feature, art activities are easily incorporated into existing lesson plans. The topical index is also an invaluable tool when creating your own curriculum or lesson plans. The Games section and Fingerplays and Action Rhymes section can also be used with a wide range of topics.

Each art activity page is laid out in an easy-to-use format. The Basic Activity section gives directions for the most fundamental skills, using the least amount of time. The Activity Extensions develop the basic activity for both more advanced skills and a greater length of time. The Related Topics box is useful when you need to coordinate activities with themes. This section is also cross-referenced with the Topical Index.

The games pages have general directions at the beginning of each game. Games involving step-by-step directions are clearly indicated. The action rhymes and fingerplays pages provide italicized directions. The spoken rhymes are in regular type.

Freeing the Child's Creativity

Each individual has creative potential. Young children develop this potential when they become involved in art activities. Because they are not bound by preconceived ideas about how something should be done, they bring imagination and ingenuity to their work. Children who are given the freedom to create experience the thrill of discovery which is the foundation of learning. There is an adage about learning which states:

> I hear and I forget;
> I see and I remember;
> I do and I understand.

Art activities provide opportunities for children to learn and understand by doing.

The artistic skills of preschool children depend mainly on the experience they have had with crayons, scissors and related materials. Whatever their stage of development, children need to be accepted as they are and allowed to develop skills at their own pace. For art activities to be positive learning experiences, children need time to experiment with the materials and find their own way of doing things. This requires a good deal of patience on your part while working with them.

If the goal is to create something specific, children need to see a model so they understand what they are trying to make. When showing children a model, make it clear that what you have done is *your* work. Emphasize that people do things in their own way. Once you have shown your work, it is a good idea to put it out of sight before the children begin their own creations. This encourages them to be inventive rather than just trying to copy what you have done.

Some of the activities in this book involve the use of patterns. This should not necessarily discourage creativity. Suggestions are always given for ways children can personalize their work so that they can create something uniquely their own. Depending on the skill levels of your group, you may need to precut patterns for some children.

When children need assistance, try not to do the work for them. Instead, help them develop the skills necessary to do the work themselves. A good way to offer help is to work as partners. For example:

> "I'll fold the paper. You press it down."
> "You draw the picture. I'll show you how to paste it."
> "I'll hold the string. You cut it with the scissors."
> "You paint the boxes. I'll help fasten them together."

If you give a child the opportunity to work with art materials you will have the pleasure of watching the child's skills develop and creativity blossom. And the child who is given the opportunity to create is able to say with considerable pride and a smile of satisfaction, "Look what I made!"

Arts and Crafts Basics

Junk Box Treasure

Some of the most delightful art projects are made from things that you might otherwise throw away. Saving these "throw-aways" in a junk box will provide you with a rich source of materials that you and the children can put to creative use. The following list will help you get started collecting your own unique junk box treasure.

For collages:
- magazines, seed catalogs, other catalogs
- wood—lumber yard scraps, Tinker Toys and Lincoln Logs, dowels cut into pieces
- fabric scraps and sewing notions—rickrack, binding, braid, buttons, fringe, tassels, yarn
- nature objects—leaves, twigs, pebbles, seeds, pods, seashells

For puppets:
- old socks
- old gloves
- fabric scraps and sewing notions

For constructions:
- tubes and cylinders—cores from paper towels and other paper products, juice cans, potato chip containers, straws
- boxes or cartons—milk, egg, cereal and other food products, tissue, shoe, toothpaste, cosmetics
- other—second use paper cups and trays, snap-on lids, spools

Fasteners

The following materials are useful for securing objects to various materials. You may want to keep them on-hand in an arts and crafts supply box.
- Glue
- Paste
- Glue stick
- Clear tape
- Double-sided tape
- Duct tape
- Masking tape
- Paper fasteners
- Paper clips
- Rubber bands
- Metal clips
- Peel and stick labels
- Decorative stickers
- Clothespins
- Yarn, string, ribbon, and thread

Line and Design

From the first time children pick up a crayon and scribble, they are working with line and design. Over time and with experience their skills develop. They try to make the lines they have drawn represent something—a house, a person, an animal, a tree. Sometimes children discover for themselves the way line can be used to depict mountains or somersaults or rain. Other times they need to be shown the various uses of line in their artwork.

rain

snow

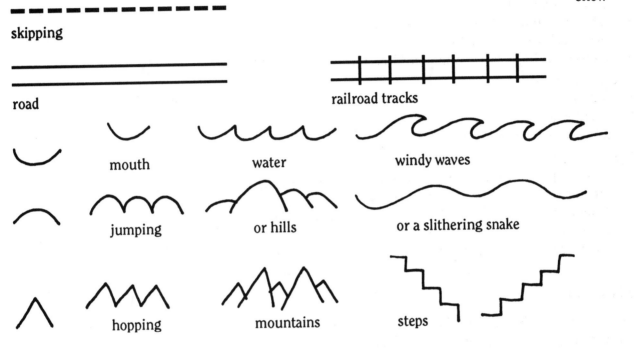

skipping

road

railroad tracks

mouth

water

windy waves

jumping

or hills

or a slithering snake

hopping

mountains

steps

They can also learn to recognize patterns in jewelry and fabric. The following examples are just a few of the ways that line can be used and worked into design.

Making Paper Shapes

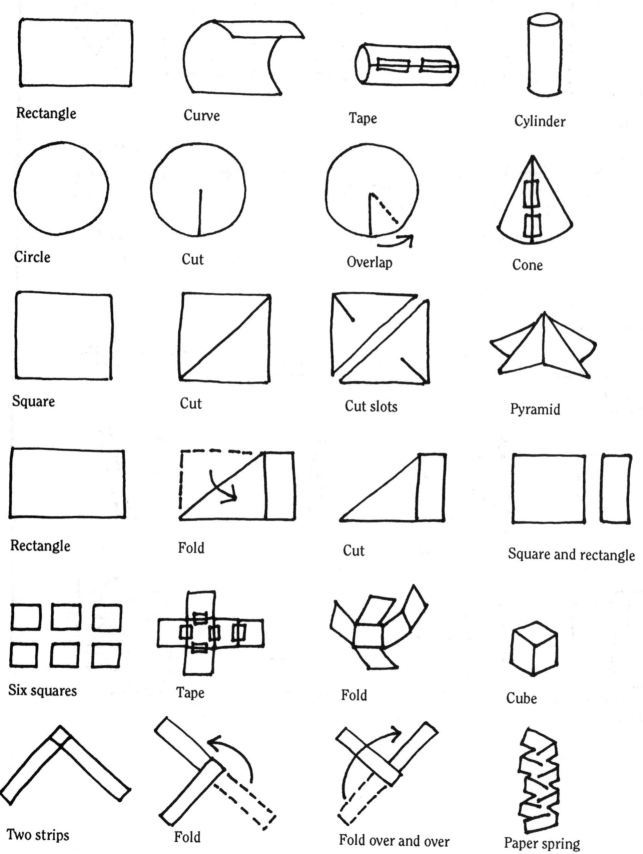

Rectangle

Curve

Tape

Cylinder

Circle

Cut

Overlap

Cone

Square

Cut

Cut slots

Pyramid

Rectangle

Fold

Cut

Square and rectangle

Six squares

Tape

Fold

Cube

Two strips

Fold

Fold over and over

Paper spring

8

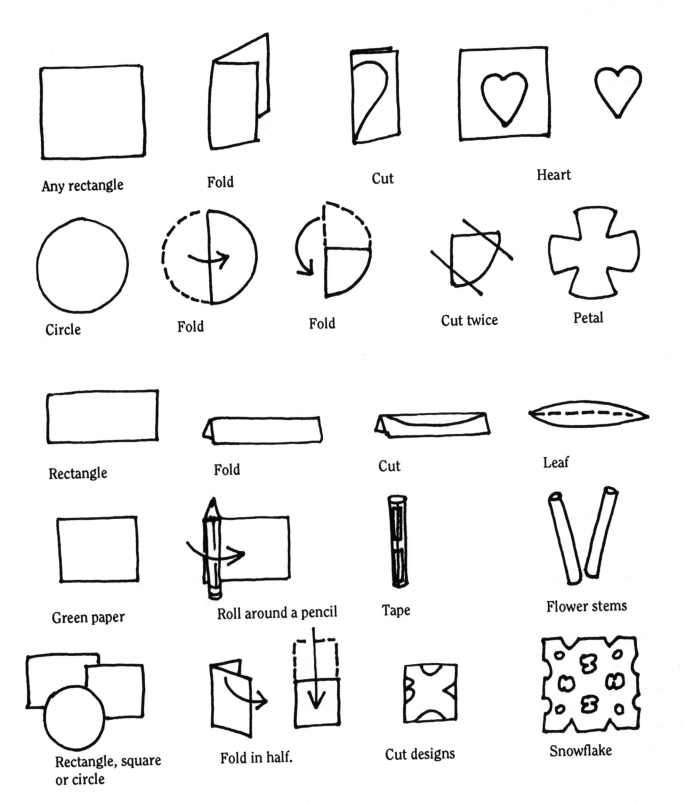

Any rectangle Fold Cut Heart

Circle Fold Fold Cut twice Petal

Rectangle Fold Cut Leaf

Green paper Roll around a pencil Tape Flower stems

Rectangle, square or circle Fold in half. Cut designs Snowflake

Folding Paper

Partial fold

Half-fold

Letter fold

Gatefold

Unequal gatefold

Single Z-fold

Accordian fold

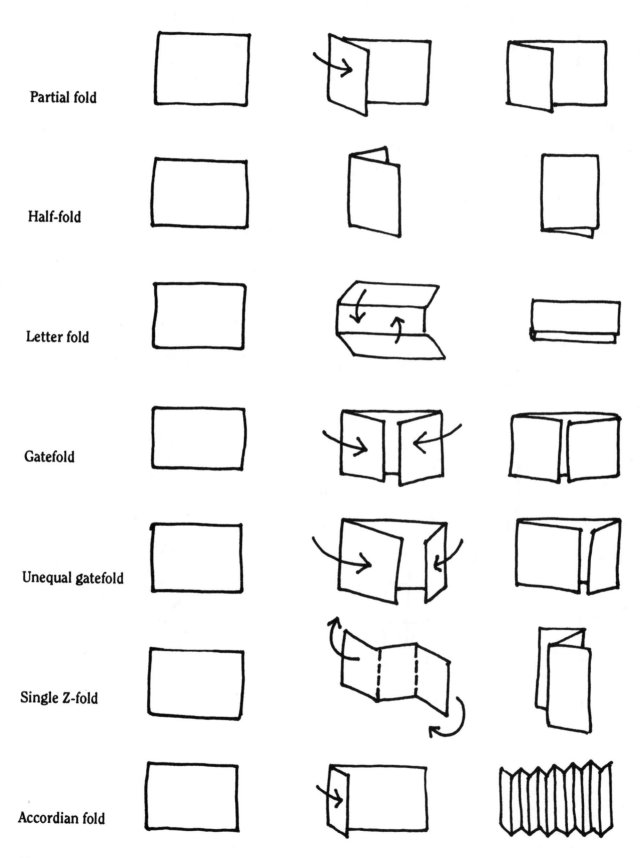

ALPHABETICAL INDEX

TOPICAL INDEX

Advent Wreath

Basic Activity

Materials needed

green, purple, and yellow construction paper
green tissue paper
paste or tape
scissors

1. Cut a 9" x 12" sheet of green construction paper into a wreath shape.
2. Cut four strips of purple construction paper for candles.
3. Cut flames from yellow construction paper.
4. Paste or tape the flames on top of the candles.
5. Fold the bottoms of the candles and cut them in the middle. Spread the two halves apart and paste or tape them onto the wreath.
6. Tear and crumple pieces of green tissue paper. Paste them all around the wreath.

Activity Extensions

Additional materials

white construction paper
Christmas objects

- Construct a white candle, sometimes called a Christ Candle, to stand in the center of the wreath.
- Make a place mat on which to display the wreath.
- Add Christmas objects to the wreath as decoration.

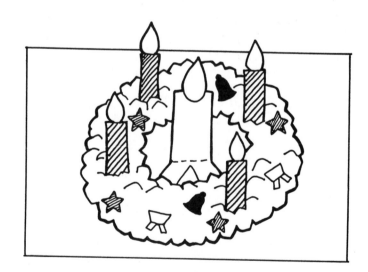

Related topics
Advent
waiting
symbols

Bird Mobile

Basic Activity

Materials needed
construction paper
scissors
string or thread
tape
crayons or markers

1. Cut out birds from the pattern on page 78. You may need to pre-cut the figures for very young children.
2. Draw on eyes, wings, and beak.
3. Tape the birds to a piece of string or thread.
4. Suspend the mobile where it can hang freely.

Activity Extensions

Additional materials
paste or glue
paper or fabric scraps, feathers
coat hangers

- Color the birds completely on both sides with crayons or markers.
- Decorate the birds by gluing on bits of colored paper, fabric scraps, feathers.
- Hang birds individually from a coat hanger.

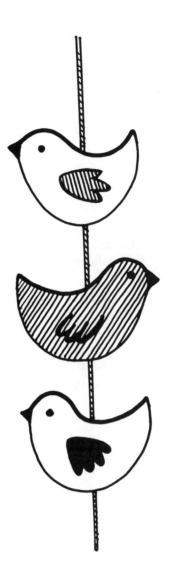

Related topics
birds
creation
environment
spring

Bird of Paradise

Basic Activity

Materials needed
paper plates
construction paper
stapler
markers
scissors

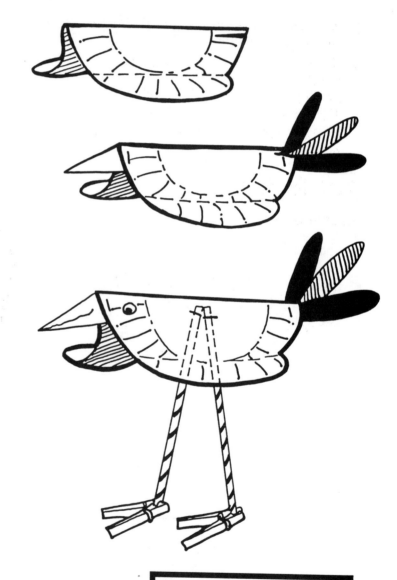

1. Fold a paper plate in half.
2. Fold up both sides of the open end of the plate to form wings.
3. Using construction paper, cut a triangle for a beak and three feather shapes.
4. Slip the beak inside one end of the folded plate and staple it in place.
5. Cut a slit (about 1") at the other end. Insert the feathers inside the folded plate and staple them in place.
6. Draw eyes with markers.

Activity Extensions

Additional materials
straws
clip clothespins
tempera or watercolor paints

- Paint the bird body with tempera or watercolors before attaching the legs.
- Insert two straws near the middle of the body and staple in place. Clip clothespins to the bottoms of the straws to make feet. The bird will now stand.

Related topics
creation
birds
environment

Brown Bag Jack-O-Lantern

Basic Activity

Materials needed
large paper bags
newspapers
yellow construction paper
paste or glue
masking tape, heavy string, or twine
scissors

1. Stuff a bag about half-full with crumpled newspaper.
2. Squeeze the sack into a pumpkin shape.
3. Wind masking tape, heavy string, or twine around the open end to form the stem.
4. Cut out eyes, nose and mouth from yellow construction paper and paste them on the pumpkin.

Activity Extension

Additional material
orange tempera paint

- Paint the pumpkin with orange tempera and allow to dry before adding the features.
- Create another face on the back of the pumpkin.

Related topic
Halloween

Butterflies

Basic Activity

Materials needed
tissue paper
peg clothespins
pipe cleaners
markers or watercolors
scissors
tape

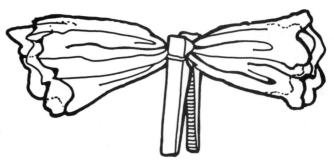

1. Cut tissue paper into pieces about 10" x 14".
2. Fold the paper in half.
3. Gather the paper at the center and wrap with clear tape. Insert paper into a peg clothespin.
4. Spread the paper to shape the wings.
5. Tape a pipe cleaner in place for the antennae.
6. Draw dots for eyes. Daub the wings with markers or watercolors.

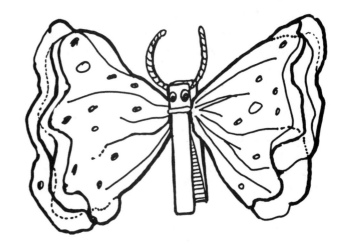

Activity Extensions

Additional materials
glue
glitter

- Use two colors of tissue paper. Place one on top of the other before taping.
- Decorate the wings with glue and glitter.
- Combine with the Caterpillar activity on the next page and talk about the transformation from caterpillar to butterfly.

Related topics
Easter
environment
spring
creation
change
symbols

Caterpillar

Basic Activity

Materials needed
construction paper
pipe cleaners
crayons or marker
paste or glue
scissors
tape

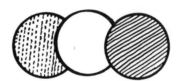

1. Cut out of construction paper, five circles about 3" in diameter.
2. Overlap circles and paste or glue them together to form the body.
3. On the second piece of paper, paste or glue the caterpillar body in place.
4. Bend a pipe cleaner and tape it in place for antennae.
5. Draw features on the first circle with crayons or markers.

Activity Extensions

Additional materials
wrapping paper or newspaper

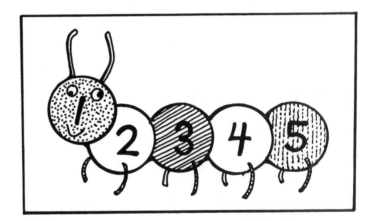

- Cut each circle from a different color. Number the circles using dark markers or crayons.
- Make this a class project by creating a large caterpillar on sheets of wrapping paper or newspaper.
- On a long sheet of paper illustrate the transformation of a caterpillar into butterfly. (See Butterflies activity on page 20.)

Related topics
waiting
Easter
symbols
color
creation
environment

Cat-in-a-Hat or Cat-at-a-Bowl

Basic Activity

Materials needed
construction paper
typing paper
paste or tape
crayons or markers

1. Cut out the pattern from page 79.
2. Arrange the pieces once yourself so the children can see how the hat and bowl are interchangeable. Be sure and put the model away before the children begin.
3. Allow plenty of time for the children to experiment with arranging the pieces.
4. When a child is satisfied with the arrangement, paste or tape the pieces in place.
5. Add features to the face with crayons or markers.

Activity Extensions

Additional materials
wallpaper scraps

* Cut the hat/bowl shapes from scraps of wallpaper.
* Give the cats names.
* Add spots or stripes to the cats and draw food in the bowl.

Related topics
shapes
pets
creativity

Christmas Tree Mobile

Basic Activity

Materials needed
green and brown construction paper
pencils
string
tape
crayons or markers
scissors

1. Draw a large triangle for a Christmas tree on green construction paper.
2. Cut out the tree. Cut it into three parts.
3. Decorate the tree with crayons or markers. (You may prefer to decorate before or after cutting.)
4. Lay out the pieces. Separate the tree parts by about 1/2" and tape a string down the center.
5. Tape a folded strip of brown construction paper at the bottom of the tree to form a trunk.
6. Hang the tree mobile from the ceiling near a radiator or heat vent.

Activity Extensions

Additional materials
star stickers
glue
glitter

- Draw Christian symbols on the tree (stars, angels, bells, candles).
- Make a star for the top or use stickers.
- Decorate with stamp prints. (See Stamp Printing, page 64.)
- Cover with glitter.

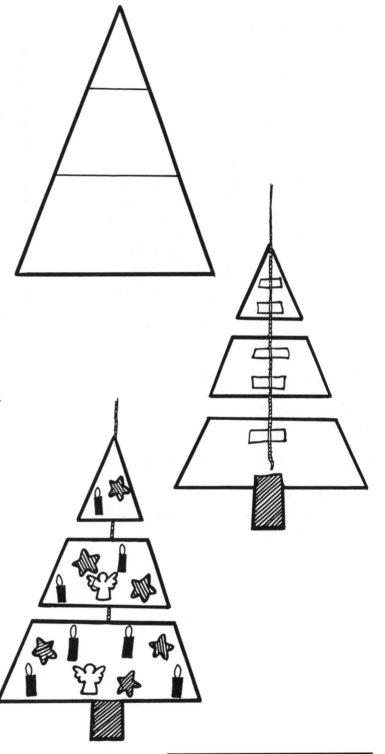

Related topics
Christmas
trees

23

Christmas Wreath

Basic Activity

Materials needed
green construction paper
green and red tissue paper
red ribbon or yarn
paste or glue
scissors

1. Cut a 9" x 12" sheet of green construction paper into a wreath shape.
2. Tear and crumple pieces of green tissue paper and glue or paste on the wreath.
3. Cut a 2" x 12" strip of red tissue paper. Fold the strip and paste or glue it at the bottom of the wreath.
4. Add a piece of ribbon, yarn, or string at the back of the wreath for hanging.

Activity Extensions

Additional materials
bells
cotton
small pine cones
typing paper or white tissue paper

- Add bells, bits of cotton, pine cones.
- Cut out paper snowflakes and attach. (See Making Paper Shapes, on page 8.)

Related topic
Christmas

24

Cloth Balloons

Basic Activity

Materials needed
construction paper
fabric scraps
string or yarn
paste
scissors

1. Cut circles from fabric. Pre-cut for young children who may not be strong enough to cut fabric.
2. Arrange the circles near the top of a piece of construction paper. Paste in place.
3. Paste on yarn or string from the bottom of the circles so they look like balloons.

Activity Extensions

Additional materials
wallpaper scraps
crayons or markers
poster board or large paper

- Make the balloons from several kinds of material—cloth, wallpaper, construction paper.
- Fold a sheet of paper in half to make a card and paste the balloons on the front. Add appropriate messages for different occasions. This card is especially appropriate for birthdays.
- Print each child's name on a balloon. Have the children arrange their balloons on a group poster or mural.

Related topics
celebration
birthdays
wind
texture
symbols

Clown Faces

Basic Activity

Materials needed
paper plates
fabric scraps
sewing notions (large buttons, rickrack, ball tassels)
scissors
paste or glue
stapler

1. Cut a triangle of cloth for the clown's hat and staple it in place at the top of the paper plate.
2. Lay out pieces of fabric and sewing notions to create the clown's face. Paste, glue, or staple the features in place.

Activity Extensions

Additional materials
lunch bag
newspaper
tempera paint

- Create faces on both sides of the plate. Make one face happy and the other face sad.
- Make a clown body using a brown paper lunch bag stuffed with newspaper and staple at the open end. Cut out feet and arms and attach.
- Paint the bag using tempera and allow to dry before stuffing.
- Use clowns in puppet play to tell what might make a clown happy or sad.

Related topics
feelings
play
celebration

Create-a-Bug

Basic Activity

Materials needed
pipe cleaners (at least four per child)
cardboard (with large corrugations for pipe cleaners)
scissors
tempera paint or watercolor markers

1. For bodies, cut out various cardboard shapes ranging from 1" to 2" wide and 2" to 6" long. (The corrugations must run across the body shapes.)
2. Paint or color the shapes.
3. Paint or draw eyes.
4. Insert pipe cleaners into the corrugation for legs and antennae.
5. Name the bugs.

Activity Extensions

Additional materials
fabric scraps, yarn, or cotton balls
buttons or pebbles

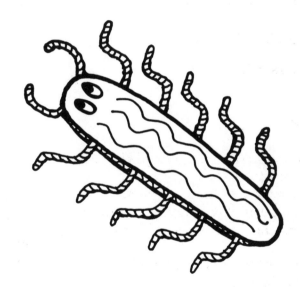

- Texture the bugs with materials such as fabric scraps, yarn, or cotton balls.
- Use buttons, pebbles, or other imaginative materials for eyes.

Related topics
play
creativity
environment
creation

Crowns

Basic Activity

Materials needed
construction paper
stapler or tape
scissors

1. Cut strips of construction paper about 5" wide.
2. Tape the strips together to make one band long enough to go around a child's head (about 22" to 24").
3. Cut out triangles from the band to form the points of the crown.
4. Size to fit the child's head and tape or staple the ends of the band together. (If using staples, cover them with tape to prevent snagging the child's hair.)

Activity Extensions

Additional materials
stickers

- Attach the leftover cut out triangles on crowns of contrasting colors.
- Add circles or stars to the points.
- Decorate the band with stickers.
- Use to tell stories about kings and queens.
- Use to celebrate special occasions.

Related topics
leaders
celebration
birthdays
symbols

Cupcake Flowers

Basic Activity

Materials needed
cupcake papers
typing or construction paper
glue or double-sided tape
markers or crayons

1. Arrange two or three cupcake papers near the top of a sheet of paper. Fasten in place with glue or tape.
2. Draw stems and leaves.

Activity Extensions

Additional materials
green construction paper
scissors
cotton balls, buttons, or paper scraps
straws
fabric or paper scraps

- Cut a 2" band of green construction paper, fringe with scissors and fasten at bottom for grass.
- Add centers to the flowers with crayons, or glue cotton balls, buttons, or colored paper circles to the middle of the cupcake papers.
- Use cupcake papers of differing colors for each flower.
- Make stems from straws and leaves from fabric or paper scraps.

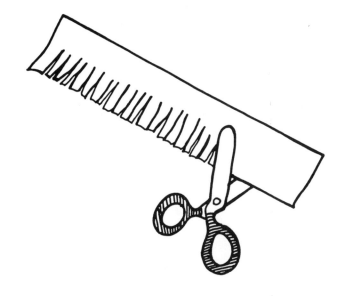

Related topics
plants
spring
environment
creation

Design Pictures

Basic Activity

Materials needed
classified advertising pages from the newspaper
construction paper
watercolors
dark crayons
scissors
paste or glue

1. Cut ad pages into pieces that are slightly larger than construction paper.
2. Color dark lines around individual ads to create rectangles of different sizes.
3. Draw repeating designs inside the rectangles. (See Line and Design on page 7.)
4. Apply a wash of color.
5. Cut out the center of a sheet of construction paper leaving about a 1" frame.
6. Paste or glue the frame over the design. Trim the edges of the design.

Activity Extension

Additional materials
watercolors

- Apply different watercolors to individual designs and rectangles.

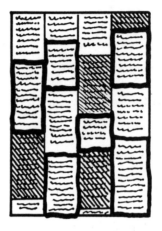 

Related topics
color
design

Dove of Peace

Basic Activity

Materials needed
white construction paper
typing paper
pencil
scissors
hole punch
string

1. Cut out a dove from the pattern on page 80. You may need to pre-cut the figure for very young children.
2. Cut a slit in the dove about 1 1/2" long for the wing.
3. Fold a sheet of typing paper in half the long way. Then unfold.
4. Accordian fold the sheet of typing paper the opposite way from which you folded the paper in half. Crease the folds firmly.
5. Fold the wing at the center and insert into the slit.
6. Punch a hole at the center of the wings and tie with a string.

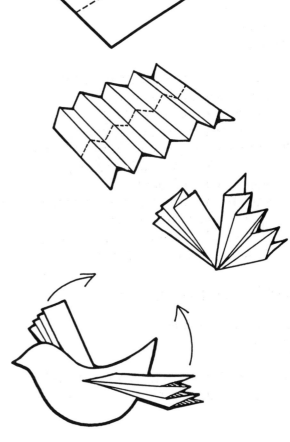

Activity Extensions

Additional materials
star stickers, sequins, or colored paper
hanger
various kinds of paper

- Add eyes made from stick-on stars, sequins, or color paper circles.
- Experiment by making the dove body and wings from different kinds of paper.
- Create a mobile of doves by attaching them to a hanger.

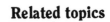

Related topics
symbols
birds
peace
creation

Easter Basket

Basic Activity

Materials needed
medium-size paper bags
construction paper
paste or glue
pencils
scissors
stapler

1. Draw rabbit ear shapes at the top of the bag.
2. Cut around the ears.
3. Cut out and paste or glue on features (ears, eyes, nose, whiskers, mouth).
4. Add a strip of tape to the tops of the ears to make the basket more tear-resistant.

Activity Extensions

Additional materials
sewing notions
cotton ball
paper for Easter eggs
1" wide cardboard strips

- Use a button or sewing notion tassel for a nose and yarn for whiskers.
- Add a cotton ball for a tail.
- Color and cut out some Easter eggs to go in the basket.
- Staple a 1" wide cardboard strip across each ear to serve as a handle.

| **Related topic** |
| Easter |

Easter Card

Basic Activity

Materials needed
construction paper
scissors
crayons or markers

1. Fold a sheet of construction paper in half.
2. Cut out the four corners in the shape of a cross.
3. Print "Happy Day" on the front.
4. Open the card and print "He is Risen"
5. Add joyous flashes of light with markers.

Activity Extensions

Additional materials
tissue paper
glue
glitter

- Paste small pieces of crushed tissue paper on the front of the card to look like flowers.
- Decorate the front of the card with glue and glitter.

Related topics
Easter
gift giving

Easter Egg Card

Basic Activity

Materials needed
construction paper
scissors
crayons or watercolors or markers.

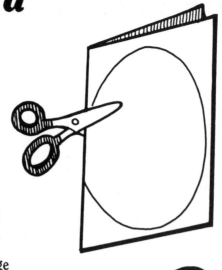

1. Fold a sheet of 9" x 11" construction paper in half.
2. Use the pattern on page 78 to draw the egg shape. Put the flat side on the folded edge.
3. Cut out the egg shape, beginning at the folded edge. Be sure to leave part of the edge uncut.
4. Decorate the outside of the egg with crayons, watercolors or markers.
5. Print the name of the person to whom the card will be given on the outside.
6. Add a message and the sender's name inside.

Activity Extensions

Additional materials
wallpaper and fabric scraps
star stickers
sewing notions
glue
crushed dyed eggshells

- Decorate cards with such materials as wallpaper scraps, star stickers, fabric scraps, sewing notions, yarn, ribbon.
- Create a mosaic with dyed, crushed eggshells and white glue.

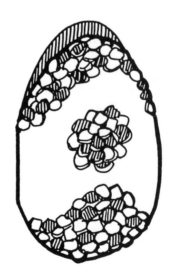

Related topics
Easter
gift giving

34

Fall Arrangement

Basic Activity

Materials needed
construction paper
fall objects (seed pods, grasses, leaves, twigs)
paste or glue
tape
scissors

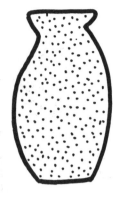

1. Cut one sheet of construction paper in the shape of a vase.
2. Arrange nature objects on the top half of a full sheet of construction paper. Tape them in place.
3. Paste or glue the vase over the stems.
5. Tape a string for hanging on the back of the construction paper.

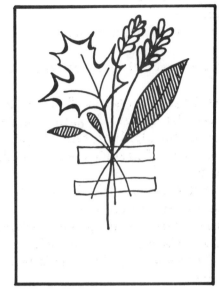

Activity Extensions

Additional materials
newspapers
heavy books for pressing
tempera paint
markers
wallpaper scraps or paper plate

- Take a nature walk to gather fall objects.
- Press and dry leaves and grasses between layers of newspaper. Let them dry for about a week.
- Paint the vase with tempera or make a design with markers.
- Cut the vase from wallpaper scraps or use one-half of a paper plate for a vase.

Related topics
fall
change
plants

Fish from Squares

Basic Activity

Materials needed
construction paper
typing paper
paste or tape
markers or crayons
scissors

1. Cut out two squares of equal size using construction paper for one and typing paper for the other.
2. Fold the square of typing paper diagonally.
3. Position the construction paper square to form a diamond shape.
4. Paste or tape the folded square on one corner of the construction paper to form the tail.
5. Draw details on both sides with markers or crayons.

Activity Extensions

Additional materials
string
stapler
kleenex
tempera paint
white paper

- Make three or four fish in different sizes. Then add strings and hang as a mobile.
- Make fat fish by cutting a third square out of construction paper. Staple the two squares on three sides. Stuff the fish with kleenex and staple the fourth side. Then add the tail.
- Tape narrow streamers to the tail and attach a string to the mouth of the fish. The fish will fly behind the children when they run.
- Create fish of various sizes. Using white paper for the bodies, paint them with bright tempera. Attach the fish to a window and it becomes an aquarium.
- Use the fish to tell a story about fish, rivers, lakes, or oceans.

Related topics
fish
water
environment
creation

36

Flower-on-a-Straw

Basic Activity

Materials needed
brightly colored construction paper
straws
cotton balls
paste or glue
tape
scissors

1. Cut four 3/4" x 6" strips of construction paper for each flower.
2. Fringe both ends of each strip.
3. Paste or glue the strips into a flower shape.
4. Paste or glue a cotton ball to the center of the flower.
5. Tape a straw to the back of the flower for the stem.

Activity Extensions

Additional materials
green paper
pencils
juice can
plaster of Paris
markers

- Cut the strips into curved petals.
- Use a contrasting color of paper for the centers.
- Form stems by wrapping green paper around a pencil. (See Making Paper Shapes on page 8.)
- Put the flower in a Lantern Flower Basket. (See page 41.)
- Decorate a juice can. After pouring in plaster of Paris, stand the flower in the can and allow the plaster to harden.

Related topics
plants
spring
gift giving
creation

Foil Pictures

Basic Activity

Materials needed
cardboard
foil
colored tissue paper
white glue
tape
string
scissors

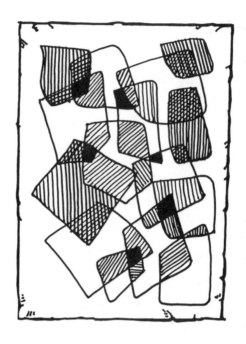

1. Cut pieces of cardboard into rectangles or circles.
2. Cut foil slightly larger than the cardboard. Glue the foil to the cardboard and fold the excess foil to the back.
3. Dip pieces of tissue paper in diluted white glue. Arrange them on the foil. Pieces may be overlapped. Allow to dry.
4. Tape a loop of string to the back for hanging.

Activity Extensions

Additional materials
string or yarn
markers
magazines

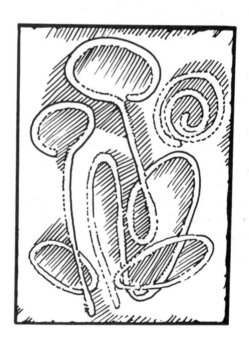

- Spread glue so that it fully covers the cardboard. Lay pieces of thick string or yarn on the glue in a random pattern. Cover the cardboard and string with a piece of foil. Press the foil down carefully so the ridges made by the yarn or string show through. Color inside the ridges with markers.
- Find pictures in magazines that fit a theme (food, animals, people). Cut out the pictures and make a collage on the foil background.

Related topics
design
gift giving
shapes

Harvest Collage

Basic Activity

Materials needed
paper plates
construction paper in fall colors
magazines or seed catalogs
paste or glue
hole punch
scissors
yarn or string

1. Cut a circle out of construction paper so that it fits inside a paper plate.
2. Paste or glue the circle in the center of the plate.
3. Cut out pictures of fruit and vegetables.
4. Paste or glue the pictures into a collage.
5. Punch a hole at the top of the plate. Add a loop of yarn or string on the back of the plate for hanging.

Activity Extensions

Additional materials
yarn
large plastic sewing needles
long shoe lace

- Punch holes around the outer rim of the paper plate and weave with colorful yarn. A long shoe lace can be used instead of needle and yarn.
- Instead of working on a paper plate, cut out two circles (one larger than the other). Paste the smaller circle inside the other, and complete the collage.

Related topics

Thanksgiving
plants
food
fall
creation
thankfulness

Helping Hands Tree

Basic Activity

Materials needed
construction paper
piece of posterboard or large paper
scissors
paste or glue
marker

1. Trace around the hands of everyone in the group, adults included.
2. Cut out the hands.
3. Draw a tree trunk on the large background paper.
4. Arrange the hands in an overlapping pattern in the shape of a tree. Paste or glue them in place.
5. Add an appropriate title such as "Our Helping Hands" or a line from scripture such as "I am the vine, you are the branches."

Activity Extensions

Additional materials
magazines

- Print each child's name on the hands.
- Surround the hands with words or pictures from magazines that describe activities in which a group of people cooperates.
- Use various colors of paper for the hands to symbolize the diversity and unity of the world's people.

Related topics
love
helping
peace
church

Lantern Flower Basket

Basic Activity

Materials needed
construction paper
pencils
masking tape
ruler
scissors
stapler
plastic jar or bottle

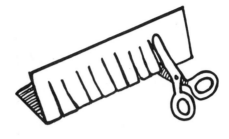

1. Fold a 9" x 12" sheet of construction paper in half lengthwise.
2. Using a ruler, draw lines about 1" apart from the folded edge, stopping about 1" from the opposite edge.
3. Cut on the lines.
4. Place strips of masking tape at the top and bottom of the cut lines to reinforce the paper.
5. Open the paper fully and fold in half the other way.
6. Overlap the open ends of the paper to form a lantern. Staple at the top and bottom.
7. Staple a 1" wide paper handle of a contrasting color to the inside of the lantern.
8. Set the lantern over a plastic jar or bottle. Compress the lantern to match the height of the container it covers.

Activity Extensions

Additional materials
crayons or markers
glue
glitter

- Before cutting the sheet of paper, draw designs on it.
- Spread white glue on the completed basket and sprinkle on glitter.
- Make the Flower on a Straw activity on page 37 and put it in the basket.

Make the Flower on a Straw activity on page 37 and put it in the basket.

Related topics
gift giving
Mother's Day
Valentine's Day

Leaf Book

Basic Activity

Materials needed
tree leaves
newspaper
a heavy book
construction paper
hole punch
paste or tape
yarn or string
crayons or markers

1. Place several kinds of tree leaves between layers of newspaper. Put a heavy book on top to keep the leaves flat. Allow leaves to dry for a week or more.
2. Select several different leaves and arrange them on pieces of paper. Leave enough room on the left-hand side of the paper for hole punches.
3. Paste or tape the leaves in place.
4. On the cover of the book, draw a tree. Print a title such as "My Leaves," "Tree Leaves," "Fall Leaves," "Mary's Book of Leaves."
5. Gather the pages, punch holes and bind with yarn or string.

Activity Extensions

- Collect the leaves during a separate nature walk.
- Print the names of individual leaves on each page.

Related topics
trees
fall
growth
change
creation
environment
plants

Lion Puppet

Basic Activity

Materials needed
lunch-size paper bags
construction paper or grocery bag
paste or glue
scissors
crayons or markers
yellow or orange construction paper

1. Cut an 8" circle from brown construction paper or grocery bag. This will be the lion's mane.
2. Fringe the mane.
3. Cut out a 5" circle from yellow or orange construction paper. This will be the lion's head.
4. Spread paste or glue on the bottom of a lunch bag. Press the mane in place.
5. Paste or glue the head in the center of the mane.
6. Cut out and paste on the large features (ears, eyes, nose, mouth).
7. Draw in whiskers.

Activity Extensions

Additional materials
yarn
various sizes of paper bags

- Add paws and a yarn tail.
- Use yarn for whiskers.
- Use bags of varying sizes to make a lion family.
- Name the lion puppet and use to tell a story involving lions.

Related topics

puppets
animals
creation
environment

Little People

Basic Activity

Materials needed
cardboard, posterboard or other stiff paper
scissors
fabric scraps
sewing notions
paste or glue
markers
yarn or string

1. Cut the body shape from the pattern on page 81. You may need to pre-cut figure for very young children.
2. Create the face by drawing in features or using scrap materials.
3. Paste or glue yarn or string into place for hair.
4. Cut out clothing from fabric scraps and paste or glue into place.
5. Decorate clothing with buttons, fringe and other sewing notions.

Activity Extensions

Additional materials
wallpaper scraps or construction paper
large piece of paper
popsicle sticks or cardboard scraps

- Substitute wallpaper or construction paper for fabric scraps.
- Arrange the finished people in a mural on a large piece of paper and hang the mural on the wall.
- Attach popsicle sticks or strips of cardboard to the bottom of the figures and use in puppet play.

Related topics
self-identity
friends
growth
puppets
play

Loopy Sculpture

Basic Activity

Materials needed
construction paper
tape
scissors

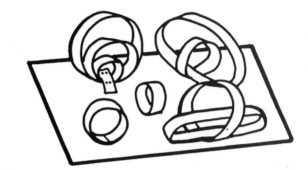

1. Cut construction paper into strips of various widths, lengths, and colors.
2. Form two or three loops, fastening them with tape.
3. Arrange the loops on a sheet of construction paper and fasten in place.
4. Add as many loops as desired.

Activity Extensions

Additional materials
pinking shears
wallpaper scraps

- Cut strips of paper with pinking shears.
- Cut strips from wallpaper scraps.
- Instead of making loops, paste the ends of the strips to the background to form arcs.
- Link some of the loops to make chains before attaching them to the sculpture.

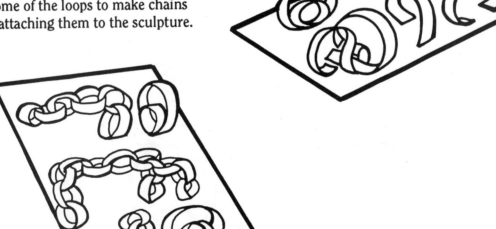

Related topics
creativity
color
design

Loopy Snowfolks

Basic Activity

Materials needed
white paper
black construction paper
pipe cleaners or straws
tape
paste or glue
string
scissors

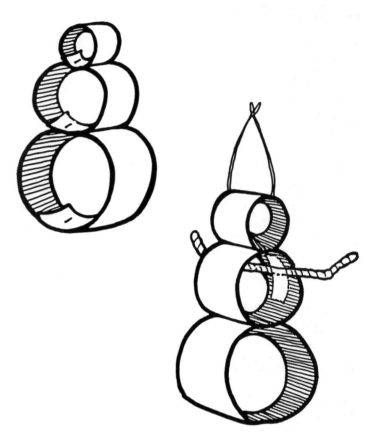

1. Cut three strips (2 1/2 " x 11", 7" and 4") of white paper.
2. Paste, glue, or tape the three strips into loops.
3. Paste, glue, or tape one loop on top of the other.
4. Cut out and paste or glue features (eyes, nose, mouth, buttons) onto the body.
5. Tape a pipe cleaner or drinking straw on the body for arms.
6. Add a string around the top loop for hanging.

Activity Extensions

Additional materials
crayons
blue or black construction paper
chalk

- Draw a winter scene on blue or black construction paper. Paste or tape the figure so that it stands upright on the winter scene.
- Draw the scene with chalk on blue paper.
- Make snowfolks of varying sizes.
- Create a snow family using different kinds of features for each figure.

Related topics
play
winter

Nativity Scene

Basic Activity

Materials needed
box large enough to fit Nativity figures
paste or tape
small pieces of cardboard
crayons or markers
scissors

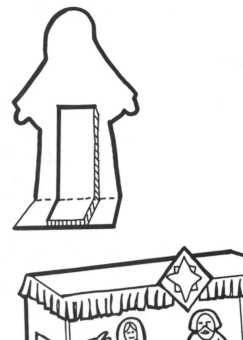

1. Cut out Nativity figures using the patterns on pages 82-84. You may need to pre-cut some figures for very young children.
2. Color the cutouts.
3. Paste or tape a small piece of cardboard on the foldover bottom of each cutout to help the figures stand.
4. Decorate the box as a stable.
5. Arrange the figures in and around the stable.

Activity Extensions

Additional materials
small boxes

- Add windows and doors to other small boxes to create the town of Bethlehem.
- Use one session to paint the boxes. Add stairs, greenery, and other accents in the next session.
- Use the figures to tell the story of Jesus' birth.

Related topics
Christmas
family

Newspaper Mouse

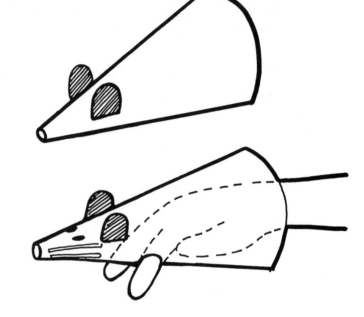

Basic Activity

Materials needed
newspaper
black or gray construction paper
black washable marker
tape
scissors

1. Roll a sheet of newspaper into a cone. Trim the end to make the cone about 10" long and then tape. (See Making Paper Shapes, page 8.)
2. Cut ears out of construction paper and tape in place near the small end of the cone.
3. Draw eyes, nose and whiskers.
4. Cut two finger holes about where the whiskers end.

Activity Extensions

Additional materials
gray or white tempera paint
pipe cleaners or black strips of paper
string

- Paint the mouse gray or white before adding features. Make whiskers from pipe cleaners or narrow strips of black paper.
- Instead of cutting finger holes, add paper feet and a string tail to the mouse.
- Use the mouse in doing the action rhyme "Hickory, Dickory, Dock" or in acting out "Three Blind Mice."

Related topics
animals
environment
creation
play

Open Door Church

Basic Activity

Materials needed
white paper
construction paper
crayons or markers
paste or glue
scissors

1. Cut out a church from the pattern on page 85. You may need to pre-cut for very young children.
2. Color the church.
3. Cut between the doors and fold them open on the dotted line.
4. Paste or glue the church onto a sheet of construction paper.
5. Print an appropriate message inside the open doors "Welcome." "We are the church." "We are God's people."

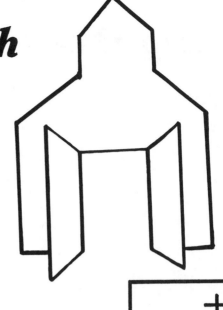

Activity Extensions

Additional materials
colored tissue paper
white glue mixture
wax paper
black marker

- Cut windows in the church. Turn the church over and work from the back. Dip colored tissue paper in white glue mixture, consisting of half glue and half water. Overlap the tissue paper pieces over the church windows. For protection, work on wax paper which can be removed from the church after the glue dries without tearing the paper. After the glue is dry, turn the church over and outline the windows with a black marker.

Related topics
church
helping
leaders

Paper Bag Owl

Basic Activity

Materials needed
newspapers
large paper bags
construction paper
paste or glue
tape or string
stapler
scissors

1. Stuff a bag about half-full of crumpled newspaper.
2. Gather the bag at the center to give the head its shape. Tape or tie a string around the center.
3. Press the corners of the top of the bag flat and staple to form the ears.
4. Cut large and small circles for the eyes. Paste or glue the smaller circle on the larger one.
5. Cut out a long triangle for the nose.
6. Paste or glue features in place.

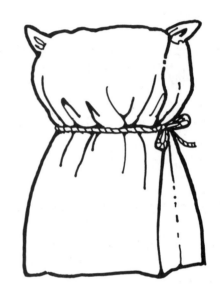

Activity Extensions

Additional materials
watercolors or markers
popsicle sticks or dowel rods

- Add feathery markings with watercolors or markers.
- Name the owl.
- Insert a short popsicle stick into the open end of the owl. Tape or tie a string around the sack to secure the stick. Use the owl as a puppet.

Related topics
birds
environment
creation
puppets
play

Paper Fox Puppet

Basic Activity

Materials needed
typing paper
scissors
drinking straws
tape
crayons or markers

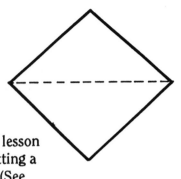

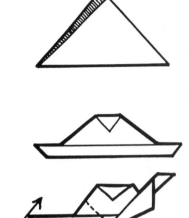

1. For young children, this might be a lesson in cooperative learning. Start by cutting a sheet of typing paper into a square. (See Making Paper Shapes on page 8.
2. Fold the paper diagonally into a large triangle.
3. Fold over 1" on the longest side and the tip of the triangle.
4. Starting from the center of the longest side, fold up the two ends diagonally to form the ears.
5. Fold the tips of the ears forward.
6. Turn the work over and add features.
7. Tape a straw in place.

Activity Extensions

Additional materials
watercolors

- Paint the fox reddish-brown with watercolors. Add whiskers and other features.
- Give the fox a name.
- Use for puppet play.

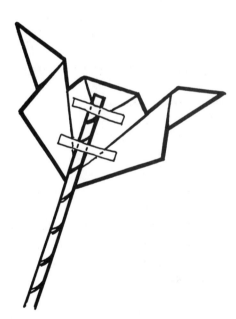

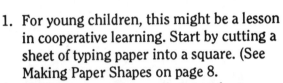

Paper Hat

Basic Activity

Materials needed
newspaper
tape

1. Fold a sheet of newspaper in half.

2. Take two corners from the fold and bring them to the center.

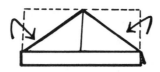

3. Fold the open edges up on both sides. You now have a very large hat.

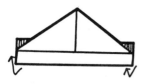 

Activity Extensions

Additional materials
construction paper

- Make smaller hats from one-half of a sheet of newspaper.
- Personalize the hat with a feather made from construction paper or the addition of a Tissue Paper Flower (See activity on page 72.)

4. To make a smaller hat, grasp at the center from both sides and open the hat. Fold it flat to form a square.

5. Fold up both sides and you now have a smaller hat.

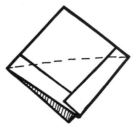 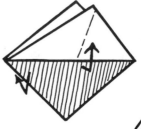 

6. To again change the shape of the hat, grasp at the center; open the hat; fold up both points about two inches.

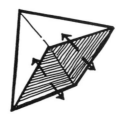 

Related topics
celebration
play
birthdays

Paper Plate Aquarium

Basic Activity

Materials needed
paper plates
clear plastic wrap
construction paper or scrap paper
string
crayons or markers
stapler or tape
scissors

1. Cut out the center from one paper plate.
2. Tape or staple clear plastic wrap on the top side of the cut plate.
3. Create small fish or other sea creatures and paste them on the top side of the other paper plate.
4. Draw waves around the creatures.
5. Tape or staple the two plates together so the water scene shows through the plate.
6. Tape or staple a loop of string on the back for hanging.

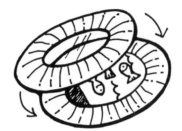

Activity Extensions

Additional materials
tempera paint or watercolors
double-sided tape

- Give the background plate a wash of blue tempera or watercolor.
- Paint the front plate with a contrasting color.
- Make the fish stand out from the background by attaching them to short accordian-folded paper springs with double-sided tape.
- Draw underwater plants on the plastic with a green marker.
- Use the activity to tell a story involving fish.

Related topics
fish
creation
water
pets

Paper Plate Fish

Basic Activity

Materials needed
paper plates
scissors
stapler or tape
crayons or markers

1. Draw a mouth on a paper plate.
2. Cut out the mouth.
3. Staple or tape the cut out piece in place for the tail.
4. Use crayons or markers to add eyes, scales, stripes or other fanciful designs to both sides.

Activity Extensions

Additional materials
pinking shears
tissue paper
glue
buttons
tempera paint
extra paper plate
newspaper
stapler

- Use pinking shears to cut the mouth.
- Cover fish with pieces of colored tissue paper using a white glue and water mixture.
- Add buttons for eyes.
- Paint the plate with tempera paint and allow to dry before cutting.
- Use two plates. Staple the edges and stuff with paper. Use one of the cutouts for a tail. Trim the other cutout in half to make fins and attach to either plate.

Related topics
fish
creation
pets
water
environment

Paper Plate Turtle

Basic Activity

Materials needed
paper plates
construction paper
crayons or markers
stapler
scissors

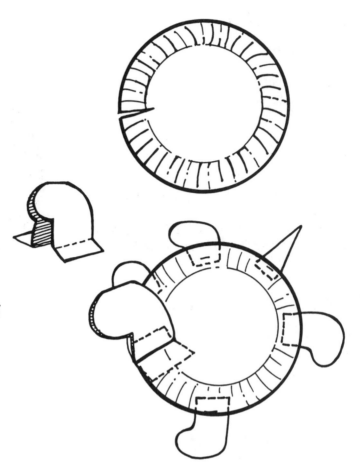

1. Use the pattern on page 88 to cut out the head and leg pieces from green or brown construction paper. You may need to pre-cut for very young children.
2. Fold the head piece in the middle as shown in the pattern.
3. Cut a slit from the edge of the paper plate. Place the head in the slit. Fold up the two ends of the head and staple to the bottom of the plate.
4. Staple the feet to the bottom of the plate.
5. Cut a tail from scrap paper and staple it to the bottom of the plate.
6. Add features to the head.
7. Color the shell with crayons or markers.

Activity Extensions

Additional materials
extra paper plate
newspaper
green and yellow tempera
black marker or tempera

- Use a second plate to form the bottom of the turtle's shell. Staple part way around the plates. Then, stuff with crushed paper and staple shut.
- Paint the top of the turtle with green tempera and the bottom with yellow. Allow to dry. Add black lines for a shell design.

Related topics
animals
water
creation
environment

Picture and a Frame

Basic Activity

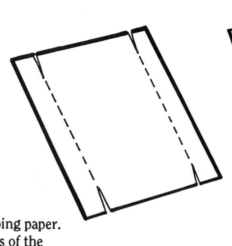
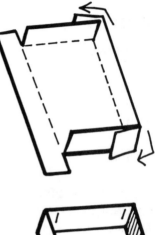

Materials needed
9"x 12" construction paper
6" x 9" typing paper
crayons or watercolors
paste or glue
tape or stapler
hole punch
string or yarn
scissors

1. Draw or paint a picture on the typing paper.
2. Fold over 1" along the longer sides of the construction paper.
3. Cut all four corners of the construction paper.
4. Fold over 1" along the other two sides.
5. Staple or tape the corners.
6. Carefully paste or glue the picture on either side of the frame.
7. Punch a hole at the top and add string or yarn for hanging.

Activity Extensions

- Create three-dimensional art by making a Tissue Paper Flower. (See page 72.) Fasten it to a sheet of paper. Draw the stem and leaves.
- Print, decorate, and frame a Bible verse.

Related topics
gift giving
creativity

Pocket Keeper

Basic Activity

Materials needed
paper plates
markers
stapler
hole punch
scissors
yarn or string

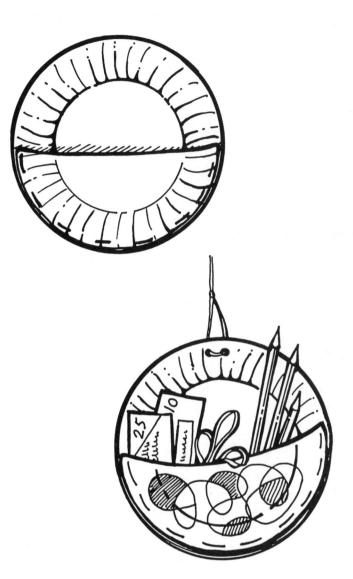

1. Cut a paper plate in half.
2. Staple one half of the plate to a whole plate to form a pocket.
3. Add a scribble design with a dark colored marker. (See Scribble Art activity on page 60.)
4. Color inside the scribble design with other colors.
5. Punch a hole at the top of the plate and add a loop of yarn or string for hanging. The pocket keeper can now be used at home for storing coupons, rubber bands, clippings, and pencils.

Activity Extensions

Additional materials
yarn or long shoestring
large plastic needle
glue
tissue paper

- Staple the pocket just once to hold it in place. Punch holes around the outer rim and then thread yarn through the holes. You can also substitute a large shoe string for threading, rather than a needle and yarn.
- Create a small Tissue Paper Flower. (See page 72.) Then attach it to the outside of the pocket.
- Decorate with a tissue paper overlay. Dip small pieces of colored tissue paper in white glue and water mixture.

Related topics
gift giving
love
helping

Pup-on-a-Stick

Basic Activity

Materials needed
typing paper
scrap cardboard
paper scraps
crayons or markers
paste or tape
scissors

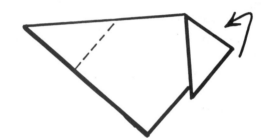

1. Cut a cardboard strip about 1 1/2" x 10" for the handle.
2. Cut typing paper into an 8 1/2" square. (See Making Paper Shapes on page 8.)
3. Fold the square diagonally.
4. Fold the two corners down to form ears.
5. Create a face for the pup by drawing or pasting on eyes, nose, mouth, tongue.
6. Paste or tape the head over the cardboard handle.

Activity Extensions

Additional materials
sewing notions

- Add a collar, a stick-out tongue, spots, button eyes, rickrack eyebrows.
- Name the pup.
- Use the pup for puppet play.

Related topics
animals
pets
growth
puppets

Scrap Garden

Basic Activity

Materials needed
paper scraps
construction paper
scissors
paste or glue
crayons or markers

1. Cut out shapes from scrap paper that roughly resemble carrots, potatoes, radishes, beets, or other vegetables that grow underground.
2. Paste or glue one-half a sheet of earth-colored paper on a full sheet of blue construction paper.
3. Paste or glue the vegetables on the earth-colored paper.
4. Paste or glue on greenery above the vegetables.
5. Draw in the sun at the top of the blue construction paper.

Activity Extensions

- Add other objects that might be underground in the garden like stones, insects, and animals.
- Divide the picture in half, showing one side with the sun and the other side with rain.
- Show the vegetables growing from seed to full plant.

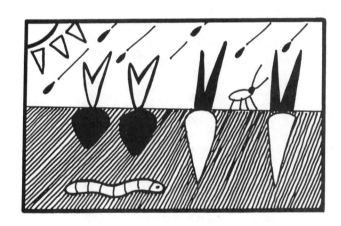

Related topics
plants
food
sun
rain
growth
environment
waiting
water

Scribble Art

Basic Activity

Materials needed
construction or typing paper
crayons

1. Use a crayon to make bold, looping lines on a piece of paper.
2. Color the spaces between the loops and lines to create an eye-catching design.

Activity Extensions

Additional material
large sheet of paper

- Frame the scribble art by pasting it to a larger sheet of paper.
- Place pictures against a window and trace the pattern on the back side of the paper.

Related topics
color
creativity

Season Tree

Basic Activity

Materials needed
background paper
brown crayon or washable marker
colored tissue paper or cotton balls
paste or glue

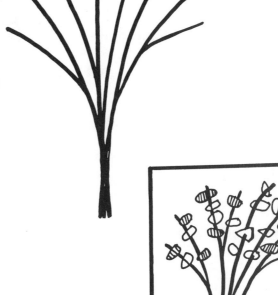

1. Sketch brown lines to create a tree with trunk and branches.
2. Tear pieces of colored tissue paper and paste or glue on the branches. The season is determined by the color of the paper that is used. Make winter trees by using colored background paper. Paste on bits of cotton balls for snow.

Activity Extensions

Additional materials
crayons or markers
tempera paint
sponges
large piece of paper

- Add blossoms, apples, and bird nests.
- Stamp print the foliage by using small pieces of sponge dipped in tempera. (See Stamp Printing activity on page 64.)
- Divide a large piece of paper into four sections. Make four different trees representing the four seasons.

Related topics
trees
seasons
plants
growth
change
creation

Shaker Music Maker

Basic Activity

Materials needed
well-rinsed plastic bottles with screw-on tops
small objects (pebbles, small coins, bells, sand)
markers or self-adhesive stickers

1. Remove any labels from the bottles before distributing.
2. Cover the bottles with stickers or decorate with markers.
3. Experiment with the sound by putting a couple small objects in a bottle and shaking it.
4. Add more objects until you are satisfied with the sound. Then screw the bottle caps on tight.

Activity Extensions

Additional materials
gift wrap ribbon

- Make a shaker for each hand and use them like maracas.
- Decorate by tying gift wrap ribbon around the neck of the container.

Related topics
celebration
sound

Spider-on-a-String

Basic Activity

Materials needed
construction paper
string
tape
crayons or markers
paste or stapler
scissors
hole punch

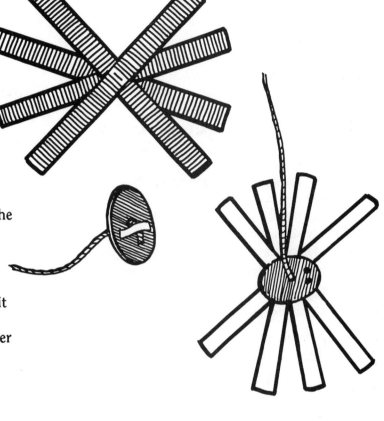

1. Cut four 1" x 12" strips of construction paper.
2. Overlap the strips and paste or staple in the center.
3. Cut out an oval body from contrasting paper.
4. Punch a hole in the center of the body. Place a string through the hole and tape it in place.
5. Paste, tape, or staple the body in the center of the legs.
6. Add eyes and other details, with crayons, markers, or paper scraps.

Activity Extensions

Additional material
large piece of paper

- Accordian fold paper legs.
- Make different sizes of spiders to form a spider family.
- Draw a large web or make one out of string. Place spiders of different sizes on it.
- Do the familiar fingerplay, "Eensy Weensy Spider."

Related topics
animals
environment
creation

Stamp Printing

Basic Activity

Materials needed
tempera paint
paper towels
shallow dish or pie plate
newspapers
plain paper
printing objects (sponge, fork, bottle cap, cork, spool, wad of paper).

1. Place several layers of paper towels in a shallow dish. Soak with tempera.
2. Press the object that is being used for printing into the paint and then onto the paper. Make practice prints on the newspapers used to protect the painting surface.

   (For less mess, use small pieces of sponge held with a clip clothespin.)

Activity Extensions

Additional materials
shelf paper or tissue paper
crayons or markers

- Stamp print shelf paper or tissue paper to use as gift wrap.
- Print with one color. After the work dries, print with a second or even a third color.
- Mix mediums. Make grass or clouds with stamp prints. Then fill out the rest of the work with crayons or markers.

Related topics
color
design
texture

Stand-up Snowman

Basic Activity

Materials needed
two sheets of white construction paper
black construction paper scraps
paste or glue
scissors

1. Fold two sheets of paper in half length-wise.
2. Make two identical snowmen from the pattern on page 86. You may need to pre-cut figures for very young children.
3. Spread paste or glue on one-half of one snowman.
4. Paste or glue the two snowmen back to back.
5. Cut out three hats from the pattern on page 86.
6. Paste the hats in place. Cut out eyes, nose, mouth and buttons and add them to the snowman.
7. After the glue or paste dries, spread the snowman out so it is standing on three edges.

Activity Extensions

Additional materials
straws or twigs

- Add features to all three sides. Faces can be made happy, sad, surprised.
- Make arms from drinking straws or twigs.

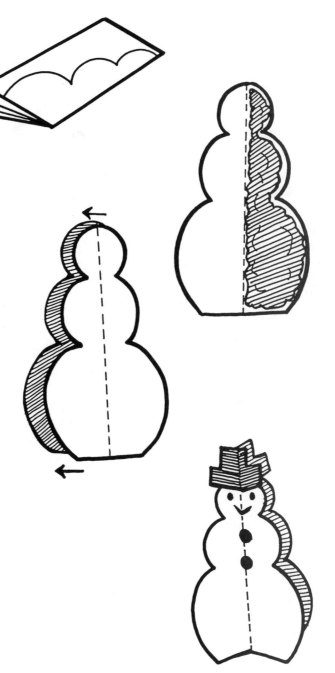

Related topics
snow
winter
feelings
play

Stand-up Christmas Tree

Basic Activity

Materials needed
two sheets of green construction paper
pencils
paste or glue
scissors

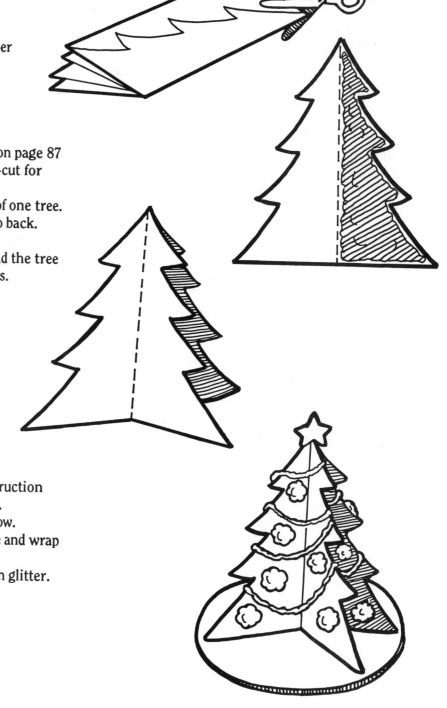

1. Fold the paper in half lengthwise.
2. Trace two trees from the pattern on page 87 and cut out. You may need to pre-cut for very young children.
3. Spread paste or glue on one-half of one tree.
4. Paste or glue the two trees back to back.
5. Decorate the tree with markers.
6. After the glue or paste dries, spread the tree out so it is standing on three edges.

Activity Extensions

Additional materials
paper scraps or aluminum foil
cotton balls
cardboard
fabric scraps
string
glitter

- Make small ornaments from construction paper or foil and attach to the tree.
- Paste on bits of cotton balls for snow.
- Attach the tree to a cardboard base and wrap a piece of fabric around the base.
- Dip string in glue and then dip it in glitter. Drape it around the tree.

Related topics
Christmas
trees

String of Hearts

Basic Activity

Materials needed
red and white construction paper
scissors
hole punch
stapler
string

1. Cut 1" x 4", 1" x 10" and 1" x 12" strips for the hearts. (Pre-cutting strips on a paper cutter gets you going faster. Do not allow children to use a paper cutter or leave one unattended near young children!)
2. Stack five strips in the following order:

   10" white
   12" red
   4" any color
   12" red
   10" white
3. Bring all the strips together at one end and staple the matched ends.
4. Taking one strip from the bottom of the stack and one from the top, loop the strips around to form the hearts. Then staple the ends.
5. Punch a hole at the top and add string for hanging.

Activity Extensions

Additional materials
red, white, and blue construction paper
star stickers

- Experiment with bands of different widths, lengths and colors.
- Use 10" red, 8" white and 6" blue for the Fourth of July. Add stick-on stars.
- Hang hearts in groups or as mobiles.

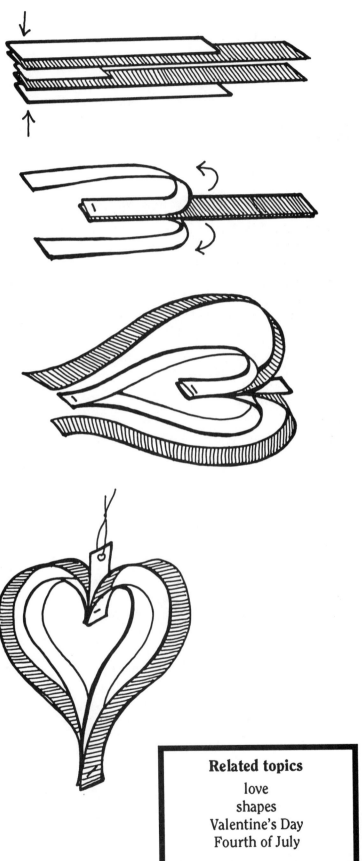

Related topics
love
shapes
Valentine's Day
Fourth of July

String Things

Basic Activity

Materials needed
boxes (toothpaste, deodorant, shoe, cereal)
scrap objects (paper towel tubes, plastic centers
from rolls of tape)
string
masking tape
markers or paper scraps

1. Select three or more items. Pick one of the
   items for the head.
2. Draw or cut out features for the face.
3. Add color or design to the boxes that will
   form the body.
4. Connect the body parts by laying string
   across the boxes and objects. Tape the string
   in place with masking tape.

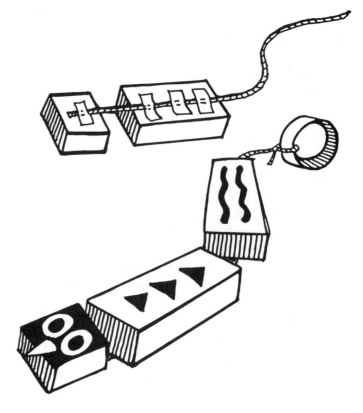

Activity Extensions

Additional materials
tempera paint
wallpaper, contact paper, or stickers
paper bags
newspaper
various kinds of boxes

- Paint the boxes during one session. Allow to
  dry and assemble them during the next
  session.
- Decorate the boxes with prepasted wallpaper
  scraps, contact paper, or stickers.
- Stuff bags with crumpled newspaper and
  use them in place of boxes or objects.
- Add other objects to make limbs.
- Make a train instead of a figure. Select boxes
  for different cars (oatmeal box for tank car;
  shoe box for a gondola; cereal box for a
  refrigerator car).

Related topics
creativity
design

Sun Picture

Basic Activity

Materials needed
construction paper
scissors
paste or glue
crayons or markers

1. Cut out one circle and several triangles from yellow, orange, and red paper.
2. Arrange a sun design on blue paper and paste or glue in place.
3. Add a line from scripture such as "Let there be light" (Genesis 13) or a prayer of thanks such as "Thank you, God, for each new day."

Activity Extensions

Additional materials
black construction paper
star stickers
white paper

- Tape a sheet of black paper and a sheet of blue paper side by side. Add moon shapes and small gold or silver stick-on stars to the black side.
- Use a white sheet of background paper. Cut out blue and black squares, sun, moon, and stars. Arrange into a paper mosaic.

Related topics
sun, moon, and stars
creation
thankfulness

69

Thanksgiving Circle Turkey

Basic Activity

Materials needed
construction paper
scissors
paste or glue
crayons or markers

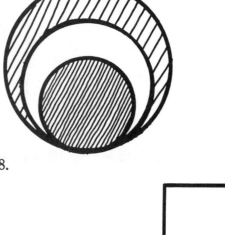

1. Cut out three circles (5", 6", 7" wide) from colorful construction paper.
2. Cut out a head from the pattern on page 88. You may need to pre-cut for very young children.
3. Paste or glue the three circles on top of each other.
4. Add the head.
5. Draw in the eye and the feet.

Activity Extensions

- Fringe the largest circle before pasting it in place.
- Snip out narrow slices to indicate feathers.
- Draw in feathers.
- Cut feather shapes from various colors of paper and paste or glue onto the largest circle.

Related topic
Thanksgiving

70

Thanksgiving Three-D Turkey

Basic Activity

Materials needed
construction paper
scissors
paste or glue
crayons or markers

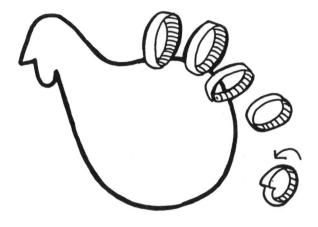

1. Using construction paper, cut out a turkey from the pattern on page 90. You may need to pre-cut for very young children.
2. Cut 1" x 12" strips of construction paper.
3. Make the strips into loops and paste or glue in an upright position on the turkey.
4. Paste or glue the turkey on another sheet of paper.
5. Draw in legs.

Activity Extensions

Additional materials
newspaper
cartoons, magazines or gift wrap

- Use newspaper for the turkey.
- Cut the strips from any colorful paper such as cartoon sections from newspapers, magazine ads, gift wrap, and comic books.

Related topic
Thanksgiving

Tissue Paper Flower

Basic Activity

Materials needed
tissue paper
construction paper
paper fasteners
scissors

1. Cut out at least four 6" circles of tissue paper for each flower.
2. Cut a small circle out of construction paper.
3. Stack the tissue circles on top of each other. Insert a paper fastener in the middle and fasten to the construction paper.
4. Beginning with the top circle of tissue paper, lift and gather each circle into a cup-like flower.

Activity Extensions

Additional materials
paste or glue
watercolors
perfume
large sheet of paper
crayons or markers

- Attach the flower to a card.
- Cut stems and leaves from construction paper and paste them to the flowers.
- Make flowers in a variety of sizes.
- Use contrasting colors of tissue paper.
- Dab flowers with watercolors and perfume.
- Add flowers to a Paper Hat. (See page 52.)
- Place all the flowers together on a large sheet of paper. Draw scenery around the flowers to create a celebration of spring.

Related topics
celebration
smell
Mother's Day
spring
plants

Tube-a-Gator

Basic Activity

Materials needed
green paper (or paper towel cylinder)
paper scraps
paper fastener
hole punch
tape
scissors
pinking shears

1. If using construction paper, make a cylinder. (See Making Paper Shapes on page 8.)
2. Angle one end of the cylinder with scissors to shape the snout.
3. Cut out the mouth with the pinking shears.
4. Punch out the eyes with a hole punch.
5. Cut out four legs from the pattern on page 89. You may need to pre-cut for very young children.
6. Cut out the tail from the pattern on page 89.
7. Punch a hole at one end of the cylinder. Attach the tail with a paper fastener.
8. Tape the legs to the bottom of the cylinder.
9. Crush the tail end of the cylinder in order to slightly raise the head.

Activity Extensions

Additional materials
markers or crayons
tempera paint

- Paint the body with tempera or decorate with markers or crayons.
- Make a pattern on the green skin using dark crayons, markers or paint.
- Paint the inside of the mouth. Add a tongue.

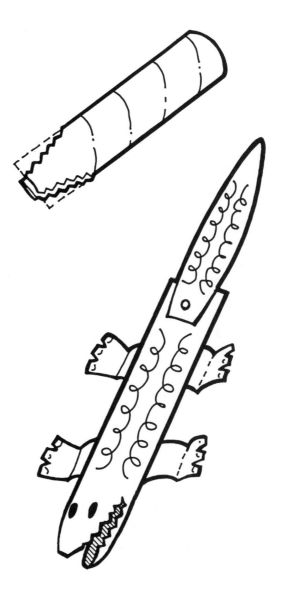

Related topics
animals
creation
water
environment

Twirlers

Basic Activity

Materials needed
tubes or cylinders (from paper towels and toilet
paper or juice cans and potato chip containers)
aluminum foil or gift wrap
ribbon
tape
invisible or black thread
scissors
paper punch

1. Cut foil or gift wrap about two inches
   longer than the tube and long enough to go
   around it.
2. Wrap foil or gift wrap around the tube. Fold
   the covering over at both ends and fasten
   the covering in place with tape. (Foil tucks
   in neatly.)
3. Spiral wrap a ribbon around the tube and
   fasten with tape at both ends.
4. Punch two holes at one end of the tube.
5. Tie a loop between the two holes. Then tie a
   length of thread in the middle of the loop
   and hang the twirler.

Activity Extensions

Additional Materials
tempera paint
star stickers
orange construction paper

- Paint tubes with tempera and allow to dry.
  Then decorate with stick-on stars.
- Use red, white, and blue paint plus stick-on
  stars. Use for the Fourth of July.
- Design the twirlers to look like candles. Add
  orange flames.
- Hang in groups of three from varying
  heights.

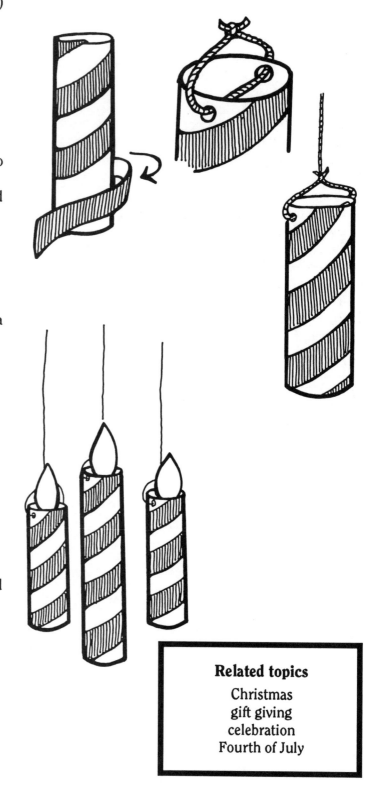

Related topics

Christmas
gift giving
celebration
Fourth of July

74

Valentine Person

Basic Activity

Materials needed
construction paper
pipe cleaners
paste or glue
crayons or markers
scissors

1. Cut out two large hearts, about 5" wide, for the body. (See Making Paper Shapes on page 8.)
2. Cut out four smaller hearts, about 1" wide, for the hands and the feet.
3. Cut out two circles, about 2" wide, for the head.
4. Bend the pipe cleaners to form legs, arms and neck.
5. Spread paste on one large heart. Place the pipe cleaners on it.
6. Place the second large heart over the pipe cleaners and press in place.
7. Paste the hands and the head on the ends of the pipe cleaners.
8. Add features to the head.

Activity Extension

• Print a message on the largest heart.

Related topics
love
Valentine's Day.

Valentine Pop-up

Basic Activity

Materials needed
red construction paper
white paper
scissors
paste or glue
crayons or markers

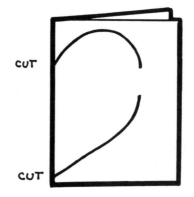

1. Fold a sheet of 9" x 12" red construction paper in half to form a greeting card.
2. Draw a half heart outline on the folded edge of the card. (See Making Paper Shapes on page 8.)
3. Cut around the outline from each end. Be sure to leave 1/2" space at the middle uncut. This will be the hinge. (If it is cut by accident, repair it with tape.)
4. Open the card and carefully press at the fold line so the fold reverses. The heart should fold inside the card and become hidden.
5. Add "To" and "From" messages inside the card.
6. Paste the back of the card to a piece of white paper.

Activity Extensions

Additional materials
white construction paper
white tempera paint

- Cut out small white hearts and paste them on the front of the card.
- Decorate the border around the heart with crayons or markers.
- Stamp print the border around the heart using white tempera.

Related topics
Valentine's Day
love
gift giving

Wind Sock Decoration

Basic Activity

Materials needed
string
construction paper
hole punch
leftover gift wrap ribbon
tape
scissors
crayons or markers

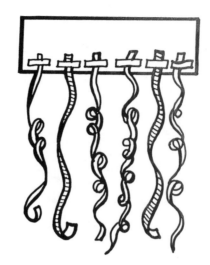

1. Cut a 4" x 12" strip of construction paper.
2. Decorate one side of the strip using crayons or markers.
3. Tape short pieces of gift wrap ribbon, about 18" to 24", to the undecorated side of the strip.
4. Roll the strip into a cylinder and fasten with tape. (See Making Paper Shapes on page 8.)
5. Punch three holes at the top of the cylinder.
6. Tie three 18" to 24" strings through the holes, knotting each string once it's through the hole. Tie all three strings at their open ends. Attach a longer string to the combined strings at the top for hanging.

Activity Extensions

Additional materials
ice cream containers
tempera, wallpaper, or stamp printed paper
crepe paper
strips of cloth
tie-dye

- For cylinders, use ice cream containers with the bottoms cut out instead of construction paper.
- Paint the containers or cover them with wallpaper or stamp-printed paper. (See Stamp Printing activity on page 64.)
- Make streamers from crepe paper.
- Make streamers from strips of cloth torn from pillow cases. Tie-dye the cloth before tearing it into strips.
- Hang the wind socks as mobiles to create a festive setting for a special occasion.

Related topics
wind
celebration
symbols

Patterns

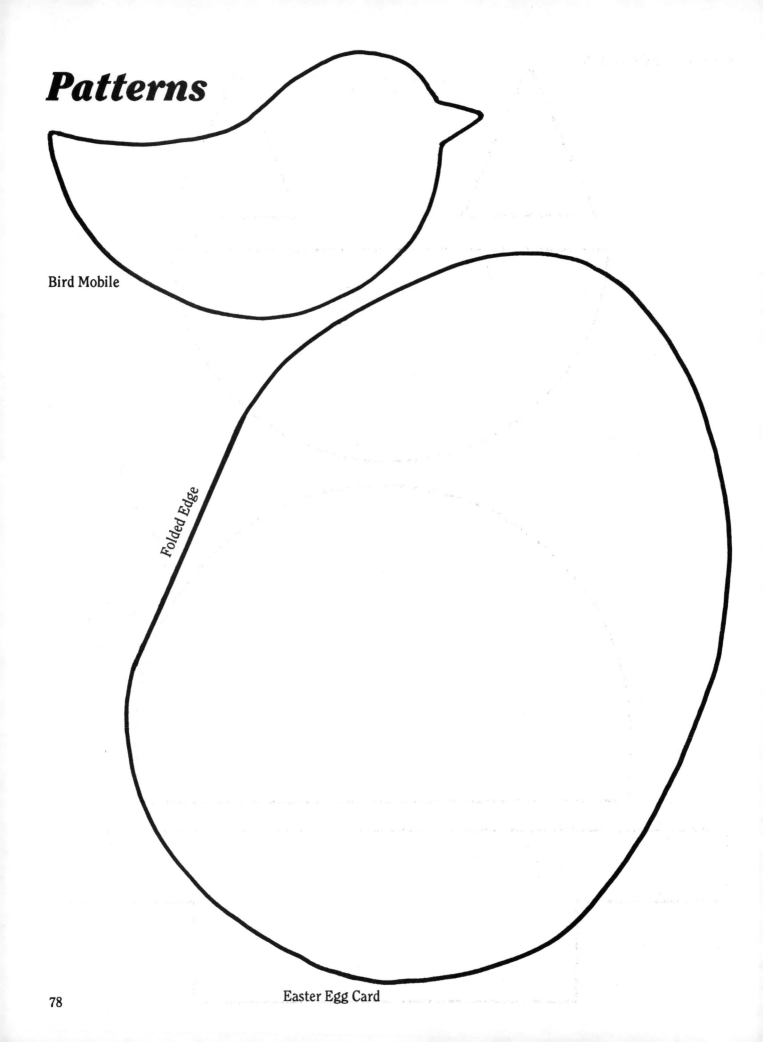

Bird Mobile

Folded Edge

Easter Egg Card

Cat-in-a-Hat or Cat-at-a-Bowl

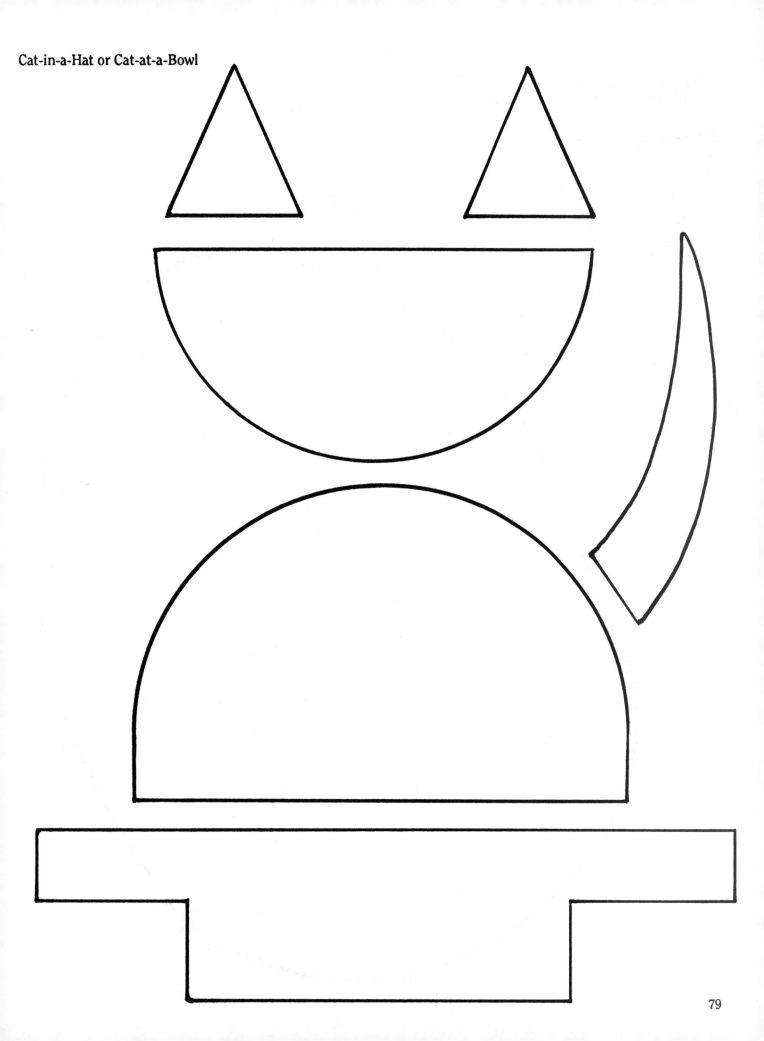

Dove of Peace

Little People

Nativity Scene

82

Nativity Scene

Open Door Church

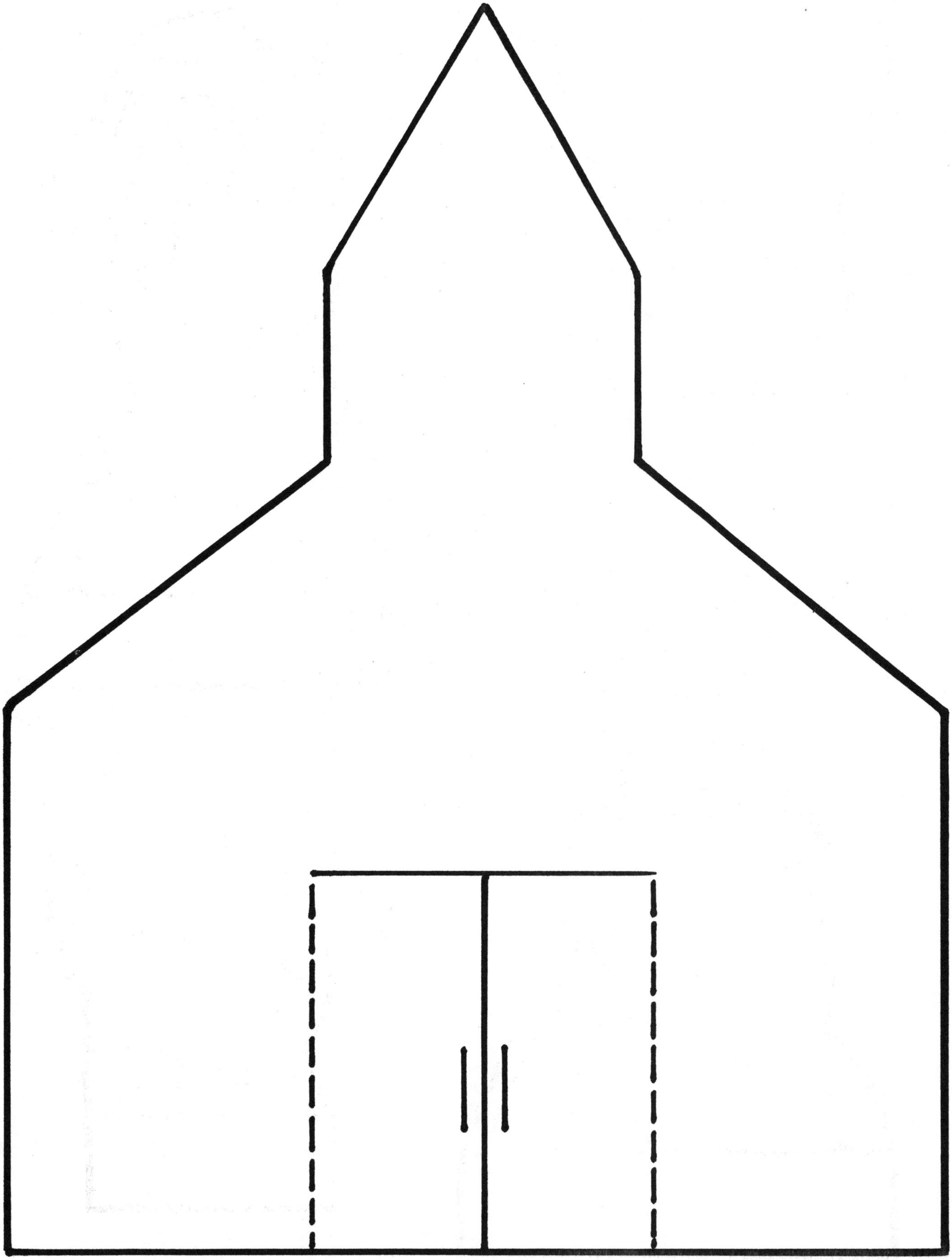

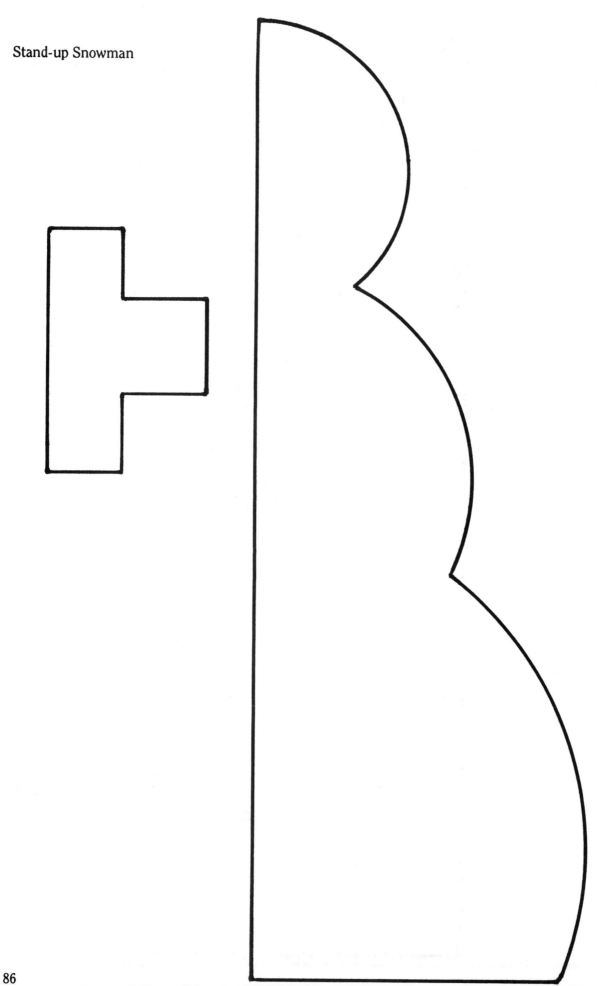

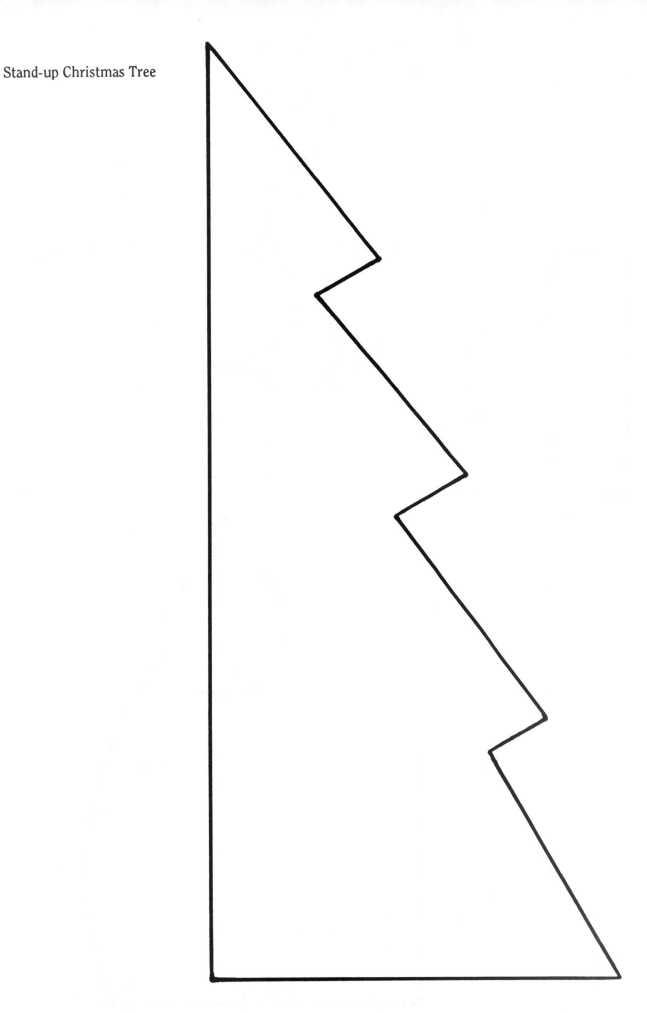

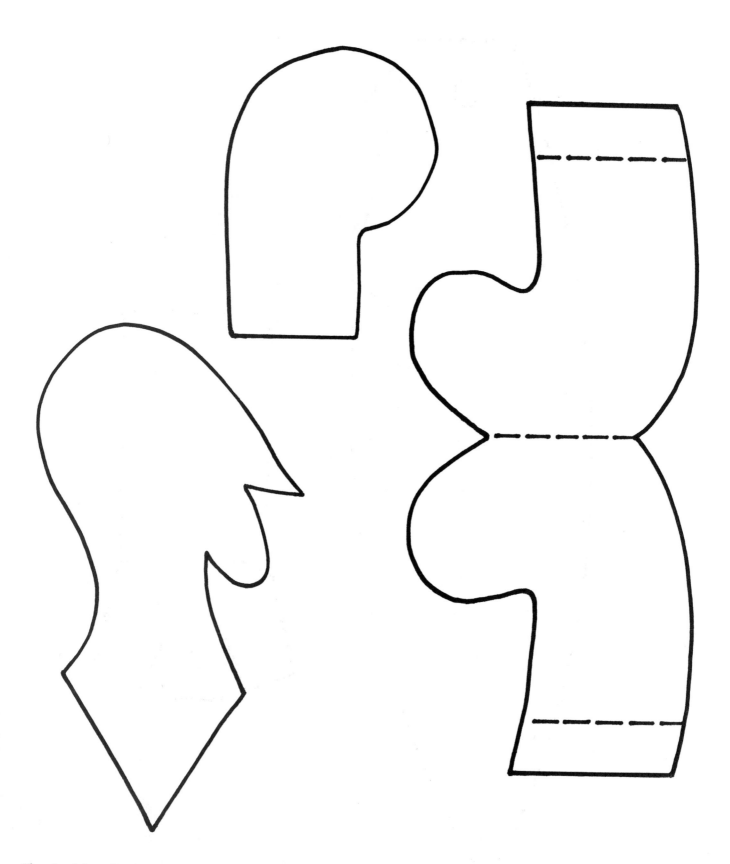

Thanksgiving Circle Turkey

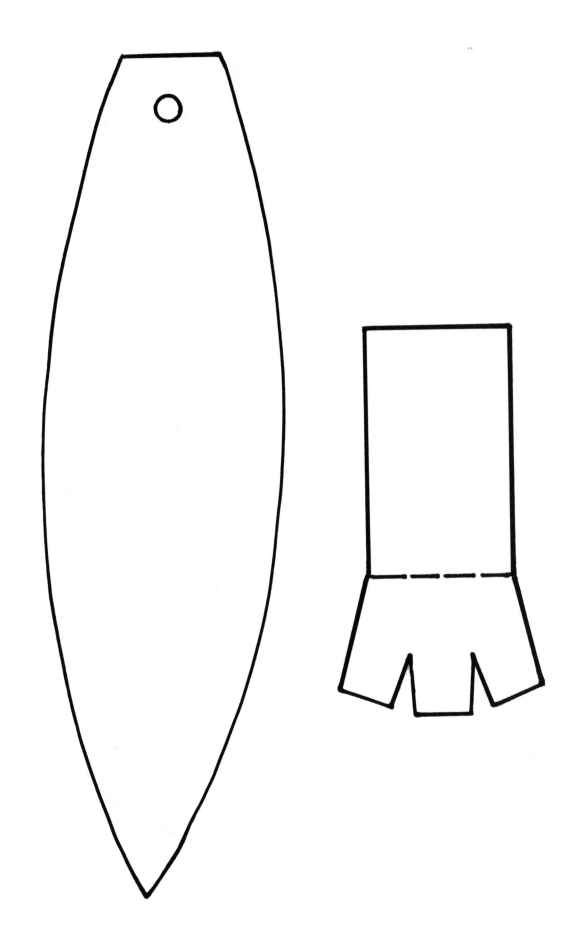

INDEX

Captain May I?

This game requires a lot of space and is best played outdoors, in a gym, or in a large classroom.

- The captain stands at one end of the playing area and the other children stand at the opposite end behind a starting line.
- The captain calls the name of each child in turn and commands them to take a certain number of giant or baby steps.
- The child named must ask, "May I?" If the child moves without asking permission, the captain sends that player back to the starting line.
- Once one of the children gets close enough to tag the captain, they become the new captain.

Charlie Over the Water

This is a very active game that children will want to play again and again.

- Children stand in a circle and join hands.
- One player stands in the middle and is Charlie.
- Children skip around the circle calling out:
  Charlie over the water,
  Charlie over the sea,
  Charlie caught a great big fish,
  But can't catch me.
- Children stoop as soon as they finish singing.
- Charlie tries to tag a child before he or she stoops.
- Charlie remains in the middle until a child is tagged. That child becomes the new Charlie. The game continues until each child has had a turn being Charlie. With very young children, if a child isn't tagged, have Charlie choose another person.

Clapping Out Rhythm

Gather the children in a circle and play music that has a well-defined beat. Clap to the rhythm and invite the children to join you. Some children may need a little help before they are able to make the clapping sound.

Color Game

This is a fun way to learn color identification. Begin the game with the following verses. Then invite children to make up their own.

If you're wearing blue, if you're wearing blue,
Put a finger on your shoe.

If you're wearing black, if you're wearing black,
Turn so we can all see your back.

If you're wearing green, if you're wearing green,
Wave your hand so you can be seen.

If you're wearing brown, if you're wearing brown,
Show us how to be a clown.

If you're wearing red, if you're wearing red,
Put two hands atop your head.

If you're wearing yellow, if you're wearing yellow,
Shake, shake, shake, like a bowl of Jello.

If you're wearing pink, if you're wearing pink,
Let us see your eyes go blink, blink, blink.

If you're wearing white, if you're wearing white,
Put your head down and say good night.

Dancing with Streamers

Each child needs a streamer or scarf about two feet long. Play music and invite the children to move freely to the rhythm and wave their streamers as they dance.

Did Anyone Move?

This is a good game for developing powers of observation.

- Everyone sits in a circle.
- One child turns away from the group and covers his or her eyes.
- The teacher moves a few children (or has everyone remain in place).
- The child turns around.
- Everyone in the circle asks: "Did anyone move?"
- The child answers yes or no.
- The teacher or child chooses the next person.

Did You Ever See a Lassie?

Children will enjoy this game involving a singsong verse.

- Children form a circle with one child in the middle.
- Children in the circle sing two questions:
  Did you ever see a lassie, a lassie, a lassie?
      (or "laddie" if it's a boy)
  Did you ever see a lassie go this way and that?
- The child in the middle answers the questions with a motion of his or her choice (clap, hop, spin, bob head).
- The other children imitate the motions as the singing continues:
  Go this way and that way?
  Go this way and that way?
  Did you ever see a lassie go this way and that?
- The child in the center stops the motion and chooses a child from the circle to go into the center.

The song is repeated until all children have been chosen.

Hide and Seek Things

This game can be used for various special occasions. Hide a Christmas card, Easter egg, or other object that is in keeping with the occasion or the theme of the lesson.

- Hide a spoon or other small object (pencil, spool, bottle cap). The object should be hidden in such a way that nothing has to be moved in order to find it.
- The children walk around looking for the object.
- When they find it, they go to their seat without pointing to, touching, or telling where the object is.
- Give clues to anyone who has trouble finding the object. The game is over when everyone has found it.

The first child to find the object gets to hide it for the next game.

Hot and Cold

Children delight in this boisterous game.

- One child turns away from the group and covers his or her eyes.
- The teacher or another child moves an object to a place where it can be seen but not easily discovered.
- The first child faces the group and searches for the object.
- When the child moves closer to the object, the group calls out, "You're warm" or "You're getting hotter," and finally, "You're burning." When the child moves away from the object, the group calls out, "You're getting cold" or "You're freezing."
- After finding the object, the child chooses the next person.

Jump Over the Hoop

This activity develops coordination and balance.

Place a hula hoop on the floor or make a circle on the floor using rope. Have children stand close to it and take turns jumping in and out, without jumping on the hoop. Children who are able to count can see how many times they are able to jump over the hoop without landing on it.

Jump Over the Rope

This game helps children develop coordination and balance.

Lay a jump rope or other piece of rope in a straight line on the floor. Have the children stand close to the rope and jump back and forth over it without landing on the rope. Children who are able to count can see how many times they are able to jump over the rope without landing on it.

Jump Up Name Game

This is a good getting acquainted game. The adult can either call out the names of the children or have the children follow the directions below.

- Children sit in a circle.
- One player begins the game by saying the name of the person to his or her right.
- The person whose name was called jumps up quickly and sits down again. That person then says the name of the person sitting to his or her right.
- The game continues until everyone has been introduced.

Just Like Me

Each child will enjoy having the rest of the group follow his or her actions.

- The teacher does a simple action (claps hands, taps toes, waves hand) while chanting, "Everybody do this, do this, do this. Everybody do this just like me."
- The children mimic whatever the teacher does.
- The verse is repeated with a different action each time. (Spin around; bow; bob head; pretend to shake a hand; stretch.)
- Children then take turns being the leader.

Leader

This is a game which involves both guessing and action.

- Everyone sits in a circle.
- The teacher chooses a child who turns away and covers his or her eyes.
- The teacher chooses someone else to be the Leader.
- The Leader begins clapping hands.
- Everyone follows what the Leader does.
- The Leader keeps changing actions. (Stamping a foot; jumping; hopping; shaking a hand.)
- The first child turns back and gets three guesses to find out who the Leader is.
- The child who was the Leader becomes the next person that guesses.

Riddle-Diddle-Dee, What Do I See?

Riddle games challenge children to look and listen. This game can be adapted to suit the environment and age of the children. Children can make up clues about things they see and have others try to guess the answer.

Riddle-diddle-dee, what do I see? I see something brown . . . it stands on legs but has no arms . . . we work on it. (table)

Riddle-diddle-dee, what do I see? I see something big . . . it has a trunk, but it is not an elephant . . . birds can make a home in it . . . . (tree)

Riddle-diddle-dee, what do I see? I see something round . . . it can roll . . . we can throw it . . . we can play a game with it. (ball)

Train

Children love to pretend. This game will encourage their use of imagination.

Children form a line with their hands on the shoulders of the person in front of them. The first child is the engine; the last child is the caboose. The others are the cars of the train. Tell the children not to let go of the person in front of them. The engine goes "chugga chugga" or "toot toot" as the train moves around the room.

You can make this a get acquainted game by naming the child who will be the engine. Then, one by one, call out the names of the children who come and join the train.

Walk the Line

Place a long piece of masking tape on the floor. Demonstrate how to walk heel to toe using your arms for balance. Invite the children to walk the line and see how far they can get without stepping off. Although this appears to be a very simple activity, it requires a lot of balance and coordination from the children.

What Am I Doing?

This activity helps children develop imagination.

- One child mimes an action (pretends to rock a baby; bat a ball; swim; tie shoelaces). He or she can also act out an animal (jump like a kangaroo; walk like an elephant; hop like a bunny). A very young child may use sounds (bark, meow, growl, oink, moo, bleat). This game can also be used to act out different faces (happy, sad) and fit in with a lesson on feelings.

- The rest of the group tries to guess what is being mimed.

- The first child to guess correctly takes the next turn.

Action Rhymes and Fingerplays

INDEX

The Counting Game

Act out the words as they are said.

One, two, *buckle* my shoe
Three, four, *knock* on the door.
Fix, six, *pick up* sticks;
Seven, eight, *stand up* straight;
Nine, ten, *ring* Big Ben;
Eleven, twelve, *dig and delve.*

Creation

This rhyme can be dramatized for an audience. Have the children draw pictures of all the named objects—sun, moon, star, hill, flower, tree, squirrel, bird, bee—and then display the pictures one by one as the objects are named in the reading.

God made the sun, the moon,
the stars we see.

Show pictures or point to the sky.

God made the hills, the flowers,
and every tree.

Show pictures or spread out arms.

God made the squirrels, the birds,
the buzzing bee.

Show pictures or act out different creatures.

And what else did God do?

God made me.
And God made you.

Point to self.
Point to others.

Thank you, God, for all creation.

Raise hands in praise.

Fishes Swimming

Fishes here, fishes there,

Hold fingers together and make swimming movements with hands.

Fishes swimming everywhere.

Move arms in a big circle while maintaining swimming movements with hands.

Swimming up, swimming down,

Make swimming movements up and down.

Fishes swimming all around.

Swing arms in large circles.

Hickory, Dickory, Dock

Hickory, dickory, dock!	*Swing one arm like a pendulum.*
The mouse ran up the clock.	*Climb fingers up arm.*
The clock struck one,	*Clap once.*
The mouse ran down,	*Run fingers down arm.*
Hickory, dickory, dock!	*Swing arm like a pendulum.*

Jack in the Box

Jack, Jack, Jack in the box,	*Squat and cover eyes.*
Shut in the darkest night.	
Jack, Jack, jump out of the box,	*Jump up and uncover eyes.*
Out in the bright sunlight.	

Little Squirrels

Five little squirrels	*Hold up hand with fingers and thumb*
Sitting on the floor,	*extended.*
One ran away,	*Fold thumb into palm.*
Then there were four.	
Four little squirrels	
Playing in a tree,	
One ran away,	*Fold one finger into palm.*
Then there were three.	
Three little squirrels	
Sitting in a shoe,	
One ran away,	*Fold another finger into palm.*
Then there were two.	
Two little squirrels	
Chewing on a bun,	
One ran away,	*Fold another finger into palm.*
Then there was one.	
One little squirrel	
Has no fun.	
He ran away,	*Put hand behind back.*
Then there were none!	

Morning Prayer

Act out the activities as directed.

It's time to wake up
and get out of bed.
So *yawn and stretch*, Sleepyhead.
Wash your face,
Then *brush your hair*
Fold your hands
and *say a prayer:*

>Thank you, God,
>for fathers and mothers.
>Thank you, God,
>for sisters and brothers.
>Be with us while we work and play.
>Help us to have a happy day.
>Amen.

My Eyes

I have two eyes,
one, two.

Point to one eye and then the other.

I can wink
and so can you.

Wink with one eye and then the other.

When my eyes are open,
I see the world so bright.

Circle eyes with thumb and first finger.
Look around.

When my eyes are closed,
I see the dark of night.

Drop hands and close eyes.

Spring

Brown bulbs sleeping
in the ground,
awake as rain falls
all around.

Squat and fold arms.

Flutter fingers for raindrops.

When the sun comes out
so warm and bright,
the green plants arise
to seek the light.

*Form the sun by making a
circle overhead with arms.
Rise and look skyward.*

Their leaves and buds unfold
and then,
the tulips bloom
because it's spring again!

Extend arms with palms up.

Raise arms with hands up.

Surprise

Furry little caterpillar
climbing up a tree,
I wonder what you're going to do.
I wonder what you'll be.

Climb fingers up arm.

Furry little caterpillar
knits its own cocoon,
crawls inside and goes to sleep
beneath the shiny moon.

*Make a busy action with fingers.
Hide the fist of one hand in the
palm of the other.*

Furry little caterpillar
hidden from our eyes,
comes out of its cocoon
and oh, what a surprise!

Cover and uncover eyes.

Look surprised.

Furry little caterpillar
is now a butterfly.
It spreads its wings of yellow
and flutters in the sky.

*Spread arms.
Flutter fingers.*

Teddy Bear

Teddy Bear, Teddy Bear, turn around.	*Turn around.*
Teddy Bear, Teddy Bear, touch the ground.	*Touch floor.*
Teddy Bear, Teddy Bear, show your shoe.	*Raise foot.*
Teddy Bear, Teddy Bear, that will do!	*Put hands at waist and bow.*
Teddy Bear, Teddy Bear, go upstairs.	*March in place.*
Teddy Bear, Teddy Bear, say your prayers.	*Fold hands.*
Teddy Bear, Teddy Bear, turn off the light.	*Snap off light.*
Teddy Bear, Teddy Bear, say good-night.	*Lay head on hands.*

Throw It, Catch It

Make throwing motion and then cup hands for catching. Repeat actions throughout.

Throw it; catch it.
Throw it; catch it.
Playing ball is fun.

Throw it; catch it.
Throw it; catch it.
Playing in the sun.

Throw it; catch it.
Throw it; catch it.
Tell me when you're done.

Throw it; catch it.
Throw it; catch it.
Our play has just begun.

Two Little Blackbirds

Two little blackbirds sitting on a hill.	*Hands behind back.*
One named Jack.	*Show one hand with thumb up.*
One named Jill.	*Show other hand with thumb up.*
Fly away Jack.	*Put first hand behind back.*
Fly away Jill.	*Put other hand behind back.*
Come back Jack.	*Show hand with thumb up.*
Come back Jill.	*Show other hand with thumb up.*

Substitute different birds, like robins, blue jays, or ducks. Animals can also be used, for example: puppies run away; rabbits hop away.

What Night Is It?

Outside it's night
and the sky is black.
Let's open the door
and peek out the crack.   *Open imaginary door and peek out.*
Overhead the moon
is big and round   *Make a circle with arms held high.*
And from somewhere I hear
a spooky sound.   *Cup hand behind ear.*
I feel so scared
I get shaky knees.   *Shake legs.*
Even though I know it's just
the wind in the trees.   *Make wind sounds.*
Up on a fence jumps
a big, black cat.   *Jump in the air.*
And above it flaps
a great big bat.   *Flap arms like wings.*
From up in a tree
I hear an owl.   *Hoot.*
Then the cat lets out
a horrible yowl.   *Make meowing sounds.*
I jump back from the door
in a terrible fright.   *Leap backward.*
But then I remember
it's Halloween night.